THE FAMILY METAPHOR IN JESUS' TEACHING

THE FAMILY METAPHOR IN JESUS' TEACHING

Gospel Imagery and Application

SECOND EDITION

Stephen Finlan

CASCADE *Books* · Eugene, Oregon

THE FAMILY METAPHOR IN JESUS' TEACHING
Gospel Imagery and Application, Second Edition

Cascade Books
An Imprint of Wipf and Stock Publishers
199 W. 8th Ave., Suite 3
Eugene, OR 97401

www.wipfandstock.com

ISBN 13: 978-1-62032-115-7

Cataloging-in-Publication data:

Stephen Finlan.

The family metaphor in Jesus' teaching: gospel imagery and application, second edition / Stephen Finlan.

xiv + 112 p.; 23 cm—Includes bibliographical references and index.

ISBN 13: 978-1-62032-115-7

1. Jesus Christ—Views on the family. 2. Jesus Christ—Family. 3. Bible. N.T.—Criticism, interpretation, etc. 4. Christian Ethics. I. Title.

BS2545.F33 F45 2012

Manufactured in the USA.

Contents

Preface

On the Historical Jesus

FOR OVER A HUNDRED years, leading scholars have argued that the Gospels cannot be considered to be precise transcripts of Jesus' sayings and deeds, that the Gospels were shaped by the hopes, the cosmology, and the faith of their individual authors. This is no longer a controversial assertion. However, a hyper-skeptical wing of scholarship has taken this to an extreme, rejecting any historical reliability for the Gospels, except possibly the crucifixion of a certain Jesus of Nazareth. More balanced scholarship recognizes this as academic dogmatism. It is simply implausible to assert that a mythological fabrication would gain a strong following among first-century Jews, who yet would insist that they were speaking of "what we have heard, what we have seen with our eyes, what we have looked at and touched with our hands" (1 John 1:1).[1] Of course, even the testimony of honest eyewitnesses is shaped and ultimately distorted through interpretation, reflection, and assignment of meaning. All human reports are colored by the viewpoint of the reporter and of the auditors.

Much of the early transmission of the traditions about Jesus was oral. James Dunn has been examining oral transmission of traditions. He stresses that, although the Gospels are not unbiased reports, they *do* reflect the real impression that Jesus made on his followers both during and after his lifetime, and that "we can tell the shape of Jesus' mission from the indelible impression he left on the lives of his first disciples."[2] Scholars have often tried to strip away everything that was created by the faith of the disciples, but that is to strip away *everything*, Dunn says: "We cannot press back through the tradition to a Jesus who did not make an impression."[3]

1. Unless otherwise noted, Scripture quotations are taken from the NRSV.
2. Dunn, *A New Perspective*, 30.
3. Ibid., 30.

We can retain skepticism about any individual saying or story, but we need to accept, Dunn argues, that anything that is *characteristic* of the Gospels was widely remembered, and so has a high likelihood of being historically valid.[4] The record is full of references to the kingdom of God, so it is "hardly possible" that Jesus did *not* teach frequently on that subject.[5] There will be eschatological justice, frequently a reversal of status, and a vindication of the faithful poor.[6]

Dunn draws upon scholarship in the field of oral traditioning, something that has been missing from academic studies of Jesus. In fact, many biblical scholars simply assumed that there was unlimited freedom for fabrication and fictionalizing in oral tradition. It turns out that the process of transmitting the deeds and sayings of sages and teachers in the Middle East is considerably more controlled than that. Oral tradition has both *"fixity* and *flexibility,"*[7] not as much fixity as fundamentalists think, and not as much flexibility as Bultmann claimed when he argued that the Gospel tradition consisted of separate fictional units fabricated for various reasons, and later assembled into the written Gospels. Neither the isolation nor the creativeness hypothesized by Bultmann can be sustained from a study of oral transmission. The best study of oral tradition in Middle Eastern villages shows that the storyteller has some leeway for creativity, but will be corrected by the audience if he varies too far from the *story as it is already known.*[8] The community itself spoke for the fixity of many details, relying on oral tradition, which itself was derived from the earliest memories of Jesus. This is how the words of teachers were—and still are—preserved and transmitted by villagers in Palestine.[9] "The stories had to be *told* and *controlled.*"[10] The idea of unrelated folkloric tales being the basis for the Gospels does not fit this model. Further, the Jesus stories were preserved in Jewish communities by people who were steeped in the Scriptures and who valued the *teaching* content. "The first life-setting of the Jesus tradition was not popular folklore and romance but a teach-and-learn situation."[11]

4. It may have been *elaborated* by the community, but is not likely to have been *invented* by the community (ibid., 70).

5. Dunn, *Jesus Remembered*, 384.

6. Ibid., 412–17.

7. Dunn, *A New Perspective*, 51.

8. Bailey, "Informal Controlled Oral Tradition," 42.

9. Ibid., 34–54.

10. Ibid., 51.

11. Riesner, "Jesus as Preacher and Teacher," 191.

Riesner probably goes too far, however, accepting the hypothesis of Gerhardsson, that Jesus formally taught his disciples to memorize his sayings.[12] Bailey provides a needed corrective when he says that transmission of Jesus sayings was *informal* rather than as *formal* as Gerhardsson posits; but also that it was *controlled* rather than *uncontrolled* (endlessly fictionalizing) as Bultmann had thought.[13] I stand by these views, even though it seems true that Dunn's and Bailey's approaches underemphasize the significance of eyewitnesses like Peter, and overvalue an alleged village setting (what about the urban house churches?).[14]

Others have observed that Jewish communities were careful about preserving the sayings of teachers, and probably used at least as much care in preserving the sayings of Jesus.[15] This is not to deny the fact that some sayings were modified, lengthened, or made to apply to something not originally intended. Form and redaction criticism do not need to be banished, but nuanced.

Another important question is how political was Jesus? It is a commonplace among many scholars today to assert that there was no separation between religion and politics in Jesus' day, so his message was fully political. This oversimplification is sometimes used to turn Jesus into an anti-Roman political agitator. But picturing Jesus as a typical patriotic Jew leaves one unable to account for his remarkable openness to Gentiles[16] or for his deliberate separation from the political debates of his day.[17] It is important "to set Jesus credibly within his historical context," to recognize him as "a first-century Jew,"[18] but this should not mean overlooking his differentiation from, and "sharp critique of his contemporaries."[19] The truism about religion and politics being intermixed in his day should not be used to make Jesus an unremarkable example of the religious politics of his time.

12. Gerhardsson, "Illuminating the Kingdom," 305–8.

13. Bailey, "Informal Controlled Oral Tradition," 40, 50.

14. Byrskog, "New Perspective," 465–67.

15. Stanton, *Gospel Truth?*, 61.

16. "In no one in Israel have I found such faith" (Matt 8:10). A remark that nearly got him killed by his fellow Nazarenes was saying that only a Phoenician and a Syrian were healed in the time of Elijah and Elisha (Luke 4:25–30). He taught in the Gentile regions of Tyre and Sidon, and the mixed but still largely Gentile territory of the Decapolis (Mark 7:24–31; 5:1; Matt 15:21; cf. Mark 3:8; John 12:20).

17. Matt 22:21; Mark 12:17; John 6:15; 18:36.

18. Wright, *Jesus and the Victory of God*, 89, 85.

19. Ibid., 98.

Current scholarship is proud of re-situating Jesus back in his Jewish environment but sometimes is insensitive to the danger of pushing him into the crowd and effacing his uniqueness. That uniqueness comes through in the text of the four canonical gospels, and this is true despite the valid academic axiom that the teachings of Jesus are not preserved verbatim but that each evangelist has imprinted his own view upon the tradition. Before such individual shaping, however, came the *group* adaptation of Jesus' message to the apocalyptic viewpoint of his immediate circle of disciples. Popular concepts became attached to Jesus' teaching early on. If we can discern the dominant ideas of his followers, then we are alerted to the earliest pattern of adaptation of his sayings. His followers assimilated his original ideas to older ones, pouring his new wine into old bottles (old ways of thinking). The remarks about *Gehenna* in Mark 9:44–48 reflect apocalyptic speculation like that seen in *1 Enoch* and later literature.[20] This does not mean that Jesus had no apocalyptic beliefs, but that it is difficult to separate them from the heightened apocalypticism of his early biographers. We see the idea of God's severe and final judgment being placed on the lips of Jesus in Matt 19:28; 16:27; Luke 22:30, but John corrects this view in a way that seems more consistent with Jesus' whole teaching: "I came not to judge the world, but to save the world" (12:47, which is consistent with "the Son of Man came to seek out and to save the lost," the "sick," the lost sheep [Luke 19:10; Matt 9:12–13; Luke 15:4]). These passages focusing on God's parental watchcare are more characteristic of Jesus' teachings than are the apocalyptic ideas attributed to him in concentrated doses in such places as Mark 13 and Matthew 24.

The tradition gives us glimpses of Jesus arguing with the basic ideas of his followers, such as their nationalistic revolutionary view,[21] and it is likely that there were many more such arguments. Partially obscured but still preserved in the NT, is the tradition of his radical re-centering of salvation in the concept of a family of God,[22] an idea that the church partially replaces

20. "To those who curse (there will be) plague and pain forever"; evil leaders will be "thrown into an abyss, full of fire and flame" (*1 Enoch* 22:11; 90:24). In the mouth of Jesus, however, *gehenna* would more accurately be translated "judgment" than "hell" (Finlan, *Options on Atonement*, 37 n. 30).

21. Mark 12:35–37; Matt 8:10–11; 26:52; John 6:15.

22. "The family model was clearly dominant for Jesus of Nazareth"; fulfilling Jesus' challenges "depends upon the presence and character of God as . . . Father" (Hellerman, *Ancient Church as Family*, 70).

with its preaching on sin, wrath, and the Messiah's death providing a kind of sacrificial deliverance.

Jesus' emphasis on humility and service was preserved, though not entirely understood. These were non-hierarchic—even anti-hierarchic—values for Jesus. True disciples were brothers who did not seek to be "the greatest in the kingdom of heaven" (Matt 18:1; cf. Luke 22:24) or to "lord it over" others while claiming to be "benefactors" (Luke 22:25)—a very accurate description of the patronage system.

Obviously, there is much more to be said about historical Jesus studies, but this should suffice to allow one to proceed on the basis of teachings that recur throughout the Gospels. While noting that each evangelist gives a certain slant to the material, we trust the historicity of teachings that remain central, even in each different Gospel portrait. God as a father, personally accessible through honest faith, is *characteristic* of Jesus' teaching (and not just the "Synoptic Jesus").[23] The core of Jesus' message is one of trust in the watchcare of the loving, parental God.

Before proceeding, I wish to point out that there is a very personal dimension to this book. Many of the truths discussed here are ones to which I need to become more wholeheartedly loyal. Others are truths by which I am passionately moved. Some of the assertions made here are strongly supported by scholarship; others are more contested. I have always written with the assumption that my readers are intelligent enough to take what they need, to do their own research, and that there is no need to alert them whenever they are approaching a highly "personal" passage.

---

23. One example of a resurgent interest in the historical value of the Gospel of John is the collection by Anderson, Just, and Thatcher, *John, Jesus, and History,* vol. 1.

Abbreviations

AJT—Asia Journal of Theology
BTB—Biblical Theology Bulletin
Chron—Chronicles (1 Chron is First Chronicles; 2 Chron is Second Chronicles)
Col—Colossians
Cor—Corinthians (1 Cor is First Corinthians; 2 Cor is Second Corinthians)
CUP—Cambridge University Press
Deut—Deuteronomy
Eph—Ephesians
Gal—Galatians
Heb—Hebrews
Isa—Isaiah
IVP—InterVarsity Press
JBL—Journal of Biblical Literature
JSNT Sup—Journal for the Study of the New Testament, Supplement Series
KJV—King James Version
LCL—Loeb Classical Library
NRSV—New Revised Standard Version
NT—New Testament
NTS—New Testament Studies
OT—Old Testament
OTL—Old Testament Library; a series of Westminster John Knox Press
OTP—The Old Testament Pseudepigrapha, 2 volumes, edited by James H. Charlesworth. New York: Doubleday, 1983.
OUP—Oxford University Press
Phil—Philippians
Phlm—Philemon
Prov—Proverbs
Ps or Pss—Psalm or Psalms

Abbreviations

Rom—Romans
RSV—Revised Standard Version
Sam—Samuel (1 Sam is First Samuel; 2 Sam is Second Samuel)
SBLSymS—Society of Biblical Literature Symposium Series
Thess—Thessalonians (1 Thess is First Thessalonians ; 2 Thess is Second Thessalonians)
Tim—Timothy (1 Tim is First Timothy ; 2 Tim is Second Timothy)
Tit—Titus
WBC—Word Biblical Commentary

ONE

"My Father and your Father"

The Gospel Principles

THE MOST NOTICEABLY CHARACTERISTIC teaching of Jesus is his focus "on the character of God, on God as a loving Father."[1] His remarkable teaching is that God is not only *his* father, but the personal and loving father of believers as well.

Jesus and Paul have quite different entrance-metaphors for salvation. Paul has an adoption metaphor (Rom 8:15; Gal 4:5), while Jesus speaks of "being born from above" (John 3:3). Adoption implies that one is not a child of God to begin with, but must be formally admitted into the family. There is a subtle but important difference in Jesus' image of a second birth, which suggests some continuity or parallel between the first birth and the second birth. One is re-born into an expanded awareness of that into which one was *first* born. Being "born of the spirit" (John 3:4) means becoming spiritually motivated—thinking and acting in accordance with one's highest grasp of interpersonal, moral, and intellectual values (loving God with all one's heart and soul and mind, Matt 22:37; Mark 12:30; Luke 10:27).

People are children of God, and simply need to activate the relationship, for "it is your Father's good pleasure to give you the kingdom" (Luke 12:32). The phrase "your Father" or "your heavenly Father" occurs fifteen times just in Matthew 5–6, and is sprinkled throughout the Synoptic Gospels. Although "Father" is common in the Gospel of John, "your Father" occurs only once, but this is a very clear statement of God as the Father of believers: "I ascend to my Father and your Father, to my God and your God" (John 20:17).[2] In this passage, Jesus places himself equal to believers,

1. Snodgrass, "Gospel of Jesus," 41–42.

2. "Your" (*hymōn*) is grammatically plural, but the individual is certainly included in these collectives.

1

as regards the fact of sonship with God. In this simple fact of sonship (not in other matters, such as having life-giving power in oneself, having existed before Abraham, etc.) we have the same relationship to God that Jesus has. Further, believers' familial relation to one another derives from that same relation to God: "You are all brethren.[3] And . . . you have one Father" (Matt 23:8–9 RSV). Obviously, this status affirms the dignity of the human person. Jesus did not consider God to be remote, but fully accessible and kindly. God is not just *the* Father, but "our Father" (Matt 6:9): he is loving and approachable.

What *kind* of father is God? At least as kindly as is a good earthly father. It is important to note that Jesus affirms the basic kindness of most parents, and suggests the greater kindness of God *on this basis*: "Is there anyone among you who, if your child asks for bread, will give a stone? Or if the child asks for a fish, will give a snake? . . . how much more will your Father in heaven give good things to those who ask him!" (Matt 7:9–11; cf. Luke 11:11–13). As any loving parent, God cares for his children, only wanting them to grow up. Jesus' Father is not a surly sultan, an angry judge, or an insecure ruler, but he takes a loving father's interest in the welfare of his children.[4] "Our Father" knows what we need, and he provides it (Matt 6:8–9, 32). Thus, our praying should mainly be a quest for God's will, for help with forgiveness and avoidance of temptation, and a simple request for our daily sustenance (Matt 6:10–15). Public displays of religiosity are futile, for "your Father" knows your true motivation, and "will reward you" (6:18). If our true Father is in heaven, then that is our true home, and we should invest our "treasure" there (Matt 6:19–21). This does not negate our responsibilities in this world, but gives us a far-sighted vision that is not focused on any worldly end.

Some readers may wonder about the gendered terminology for God. The first thing to notice is that the Father of Jesus is not the authoritarian figure of traditional cultures. Dorothy Lee identifies Jesus' Father image as "antipatriarchal"; the Father in the Gospel of John hands over authority to the Son, and then to the community (John 3:35; 5:20–22; 14:12–17; 17:17–19), very much "unlike the Roman-Hellenistic *paterfamilias*."[5] His

---

3. Here the NRSV mistranslates *adelphoi* as "students," apparently for political correctness.

4. Or a loving mother's interest, just as well.

5. Lee, "Symbol of Divine Fatherhood," 179–80.

power is in self-giving, in intimacy, not remoteness. Subservience is not expected, but intimate friendship is offered.[6]

Pamela Young points to "biblical imagery of God as a woman in labor or midwife (Isa 42:14; 49:15; Ps 22)" in order to call for "a diversity of images."[7] Of course, one could choose to substitute "heavenly Mother" for "heavenly Father" in one's thinking. What the Bible intends to depict is selfless spiritual watchcare. Diane Tennis calls for "transformation of that parent language" in order to include "mother language" for God, but she also wants to preserve "reliable father language,"[8] and pleads "do not abandon God the Father, because God as Father is a reliable male symbol in the lives of women and men."[9]

I would point out that calling God "Father" has a different *social* effect than calling God "Mother." It operates upon the problem of male avoidance of parental responsibility. Calling God a mother does not call for a transformation of motherhood in the same way that calling God a father demands a transformation of human fatherhood. The "fatherhood of God" notion heightens the spiritual valuation of the fatherhood assignment and sharpens the consciousness of responsibility. "A reliable Father God is a source of calling men into fathering."[10] The ancient Jews knew this. In comparison with the "weak and ineffective" father-gods of the ancient Near East, the Bible pictured "a unique *father*-God who is compassionately . . . concerned with the welfare of his children," and this led to a heightened seriousness about "the role of human fathering."[11]

This momentum is carried further by Jesus' teaching of a loving heavenly Father. Earthly fathers benefit from hearing that parenting is a *godly* responsibility. Having more *inherently* nurturing qualities, mothers generally do not need an extra nudge to nurture.[12] Fathers do. "Fathers must be carefully and deliberately integrated into the institution of marriage."[13] This is not to say that women are already perfect or have no need for religious values or for education in parenting. It is merely to observe that in humans,

6. John 10:17; 14:17–23; 15:9–17; Lee, "Symbol of Divine Fatherhood," 181.

7. Young, "The Fatherhood of God," 199–200.

8. Tennis, *Is God the Only Reliable Father?*, 34.

9. Ibid., 9.

10. Ibid.

11. Miller, *Calling God "Father,"* 91–92.

12. Browning, *Equality and the Family*, 119, 325–26, 340.

13. Pope, "Place of Evolutionary Psychology," 63.

as in all mammals, mothers are far more consistent in manifesting strong attachment to, and concern for, their young than are fathers. Without the values that come from culture (usually *religious* values), men have a tendency "toward paternal abandonment and sexual irresponsibility."[14] It was *necessary* to give the warning, "Take care that you do not despise one of these little ones" (Matt 18:10).

The ethics of fatherhood depend on the internalization of cultural values. The Fatherhood of God concept promotes a strong cultural valuation of responsibility toward children. Abandonment of such responsibility is a betrayal of the Gospel. Of course, the *nature* of the religious consciousness determines the *quality* of parenting (for mothers as well as for fathers). Religious ideologies that argue for strict male supremacy and control are based upon insecurity, and lead to patterns of abuse. The household codes in the Pastoral Epistles embody a male-dominant ideology that demands the submission of wives and slaves (1 Tim 2:8–15; 6:1–9; Tit 2:1–10). The vast majority of critical scholars do not believe that Paul wrote these letters, which represent the conservative (and victorious) wing among Paul's successors. They create a "Paul" who gives authoritarian advice about people who "must be silenced," who ought to be "submissive to their husbands" (Tit 1:11; 2:5), who attacks teachers who "captivate silly women" (2 Tim 3:6), and says "tell slaves to be submissive" (Tit 2:9). The household code in Ephesians does not go so far (Eph 5:21–6:9), but proceeds partway down this conservative road. Ephesians is much closer to Paul's viewpoint than are the Pastorals, but the majority of scholars also consider Ephesians to be deutero-Pauline.

In passages that are undisputedly Paul's, there is one single verse, 1 Cor 11:3, that seems to accept the common view of man as head of the household. It is highly unlikely, in the view of many scholars, that Paul wrote what we now have as 1 Cor 14:34–35: "women should be silent in the churches . . . it is shameful for a woman to speak in church." Those verses are absent from some ancient manuscripts and occur in different locations in other manuscripts. They contradict and interrupt Paul's remark that *all* can prophesy in the church (14:31).[15] Further, vv. 34–35 are inconsistent with Paul's frequent reference to women leaders and even apostles (Rom 16:1–5, 7 [apostle]; 1 Cor 1:11; 16:19; Phil 4:1–3).[16] On the other hand,

14. Blankenhorn, "Foreword: The Person of the Father," xiii.

15. See Horrell, *Social Ethos of the Corinthian Correspondence*, 186–91.

16. Paul's attitude will be taken up again in chapter 4.

there is considerable basis in Paul, Jesus, and the OT prophets, for an ethic of equal regard and respect between the parents,[17] and for "an ethic of male servanthood."[18]

Christians are having to face the fact that there are some widely varying ideologies in the Bible on every subject, including family life. We live in a time when Christians need to utilize a critical approach to the Bible, using intelligence as well as spirituality in choosing to draw upon some passages more than others. The ethics of family life can benefit from a thoughtful and critical approach to the Bible, linked with a vital spirituality that is confident about fundamental values. There is no religious message more supportive of healthy family life than the message of God as a loving parent, and of earthly families as a microcosm of the universal family under divine parentage (see chapters 3–4.)

What we establish in this chapter is the nature of the believer's relationship to God. Jesus continually returns to the image and reality of the child, to illustrate the attitude that is needed. No one enters the kingdom of heaven without the honesty and humility of a child. Jesus dramatically puts a child in front of the apostles and says "Truly I tell you, unless you change and become like children, you will never enter the kingdom of heaven" (Matt 18:3). He is not recommending a childlike mentality, but a child's *receptivity* to goodness: "receive the kingdom of God as a little child" (Mark 10:15). This openness is the quality that Jesus makes central. By affirming the fundamental goodness of the child, Jesus implies a foundational goodness—or at least a potential *receptiveness* to goodness—in all humans, although many adults must "change" to become "humble like this child" (Matt 18:3–4), must undergo a life change comparable to being "born from above" (John 3:3) or "born again" (KJV), discovering spiritual motivation as something new. Jesus rebuked the disciples for turning away children from him (Mark 10:13–14). When the apostles were arguing about "who was the greatest," Jesus held up a child as an example (Mark 9:34–37).

By founding the kingdom upon the image of the child, Jesus forever raises the spiritual valuation of children (although this was often forgotten by later Christians). Welcoming the child is welcoming Jesus (Matt 18:5), while the *worst* thing is to "put a stumbling block before one of these little ones" (18:6). Children seem to be already in the kingdom: "It is to such as these that the kingdom of God belongs" (Luke 18:16). Jesus' family images

17. Browning, *Equality and the Family*, 308–10, 368–69.
18. Ibid., 309; see also 44, 122, 172, 256, 386.

forever—and simultaneously—change the focus of religion and the ethics of family life and yoke the two together in a permanent relationship. What he says to Mary and to John Zebedee ("Woman, behold, your son . . . Behold, your mother," John 19:26–27 NAB) is also what he says to religion and the family: You—religion! Behold your patterns and obligations in the family. You—family! Behold your indebtedness to religious values.

When Jesus recommends visiting the sick and feeding the hungry, he equates it to showing kindness to himself and to *his* family: "just as you did it to one of the least of these who are members of my family, you did it to me" (Matt 25:40).

There is nothing more unnatural and unsavory than a religious structure that uses Jesus' name but puts hierarchy or ritual or dogmatism central instead of Jesus' own stress on personal trust, familial ethics, and spiritual growth. How can hierarchy be central if "you are all brothers" (Matt 23:8 NAB)? How can ritualism be central, if "the sabbath was made for humankind, and not humankind for the sabbath" (Mark 2:27), and "justice and the love of God" are more important than ritual tithing (Luke 11:42)? How can dogmatism be central if the simplicity of the child (who can understand kindness but not dogma) is central?

When Jesus asks "Where is your faith?" (Luke 8:25), he is referring to trust, not to intellectual dogmas. When he told people "your faith has made you well"[19] or "your faith has saved you"[20] he made no reference to his coming death or to such interpretations as later theology would apply to his death. Salvation by faith was *already available*, as far as Jesus was concerned, before he was murdered. He knew what was coming for him, and warned his apostles about it,[21] but did not link salvation to the death, only using the occasion to warn his disciples of the disappointment they would be experiencing and to predict his resurrection. This is what the Gospel record gives us. If one wishes to say that these accounts were manufactured by the church after the fact, one must ask why the church did not insert its developing atonement theology, or link salvation in any way to the coming

19. Matt 9:22; Mark 5:34; 10:52; Luke 8:48; 17:19. See next footnote.

20. Luke 7:50; 18:42. Actually, the same Greek underlies both "made well" (previous footnote) and "saved." *Sesōken* refers to getting well, being healed, or having one's life preserved ("saved").

21. Mark 8:31; 9:31; 10:33–34; Luke 18:31–33. The statements are factual ("The Son of Man is to be betrayed into human hands, and they will kill him, and three days after being killed, he will rise again," Mark 9:31) but they impose no interpretation upon the death.

death? The fact is, the evangelists largely avoid retrojecting issues of burning importance in their own day into the Gospel record. This remarkable restraint allows the personality of Jesus to shine through, more than scholars of the form-critical school were willing to acknowledge.

Faith, in Jesus' teaching, is not doctrinal and does not concern a substitutionary death but is a free and voluntary trust in the goodness of God. Such trust is saving, even healing. Faith is a powerful yet essentially simple, childlike trust in the Father's personal watchcare. The Gospel record indicates that Jesus demonstrated this in his own practice, both in his calm and confident demeanor before the crowds, including his enemies, and in his dignified behavior on the way to the cross, where he showed his usual consideration for others (Luke 23:28 [concern for the mothers], 34 [forgiveness of the ignorant], 43 [kindness to the thief]), even using it as an occasion to impart some useful lessons to his observers. His protest against being struck by a temple guard was not judgmental or resentful. He simply asked why the person resorted to violence instead of truth: "If I have spoken wrongly, testify to the wrong. But if I have spoken rightly, why do you strike me?" (John 18:23). This reveals confidence in the power of truth-telling. Truth fears nothing. In fact, if the guard has anything of truth-value to "testify," everyone should listen.

But bullies have nothing to say, and violence contributes nothing to the truth. Jesus did not become panicky or despairing, only saddened, by this indifference to truth shown by Jews and Gentiles alike, even at the temple. God cannot be hurt by any of our betrayals of truth, but it seems that God can be saddened and *our* welfare can be damaged. Only truth sets us free from our diseased patterns of thought and behavior.

Truth was the whole essence of Jesus' mission. Not only does the truth "make you free" and "free indeed," but it makes you a son (or daughter), with "a permanent place in the household" (John 8:32, 35–36). Not only is the spirit that Jesus sent called the Spirit of Truth (John 14:17; 15:26; 16:13; 1 John 4:6), but his whole mission was to reveal the truth: "For this I was born, and for this I came into the world, to testify to the truth" (John 18:37).[22] His life and teachings are a revelation of living truth; the community he creates is nurtured on truth, and love of truth is what draws people to him. Because his kingdom is not earthly his followers will not fight, but they

22. This insight is most clearly spelled out in the Johannine Gospel and letter, but honesty is the main point in many of his lessons in the Synoptics (Matt 7:21; 15:19; 23:28; Luke 6:45–46; 8:15; 16:10). The Son truly knows—and *makes* known—the Father (Matt 11:27; Luke 10:22).

listen to his voice because each of them "belongs to the truth" (18:36–37). The insincere Pilate, however, tosses off "What is truth?" (v. 38). Because he does not want to know the answer, he *cannot* know it. Truth *hunger* is the key to truth-reception (Matt 5:6; John 7:17; 7:37). Pilate sees no crime in the man, yet he caves in to the political pressure that the Sadducees are applying to him and agrees to have Jesus executed. He acts from cowardice and indifference to truth. The crowd acts from short-sighted selfishness, spurred on by their religious bosses who are terrified (more cowardice!) of this independent prophet. The soldiers act from habitual cruelty. None of them manifests love of truth.

Hatred, cowardice, and slovenliness are equally fatal, spiritually. Hostility to, fear of, and indifference to truth are equally effective in snuffing out one's own spiritual light. But love of truth gives one access to the undying fountain, to the bread of life, and it empowers one to shine forth with a spiritual light that all truth-receptive people will notice (Matt 5:16; 6:22–24). Although unreachable in this lifetime, spiritual perfection is the goal toward which we travel (Matt 5:48).

Before delving more deeply into the theology and ethics of Jesus' teaching, it will be interesting, in the next chapter, to explore a (partially) neglected aspect of Jesus' teaching: the subject of personal spiritual growth. Children are characterized by growth, so to speak of believers as *children of God* compels attention to *growth*. This is assisted by a glance at studies in developmental psychology and specifically in faith development. Most religious distortions can be viewed as failures to progress through the stages of growth.

With the assist from psychology that chapter 2 gives us, we will be well equipped in chapter 3 to dive back into the theology and ethics of the family metaphor, such as the new valuation of children and the effect upon the parenting ethic. Chapter 4 will then consider whether Jesus' and Paul's radical remarks on family contradict the family message that was seemingly established in chapters 1 and 3. Further, chapter 4 will look at non-metaphoric families in Jewish and Gentile cultures. Chapter 5 will explore marital values and the evolution of marriage. Finally, since every metaphor is a vehicle intended to convey a certain content, chapter 6 will examine the central values that Jesus intends to inculcate with his metaphors.

TWO

"First the stalk, then the head, then the full grain"

Stages of Growth

THROUGHOUT THE LAST PORTION of the previous chapter, we saw that the family concept was continually leading us toward ideas of progress, growth, adaptation. In fact, one of the obvious but often overlooked consequences of speaking of believers as *children* is that it compels an emphasis on *growth*—a characteristic feature of children. Jesus' parable of the kingdom growing as one sleeps brings out many important features of growth:

> The kingdom of God is as if someone would scatter seed on the ground, and would sleep and rise night and day, and the seed would sprout and grow, he does not know how. The earth produces of itself, first the stalk, then the head, then the full grain in the head (Mark 4:26–28).

Jesus is highlighting the fact that growth is natural (it happens *as we sleep*), is unconscious ("he does not know how," v. 27), inherent ("the earth produces of itself"), by stages ("stalk . . . head . . . grain," v. 28), and fecund (the little mustard seed growing into a great shrub, 4:31–32).

Plants grow, and young people grow, without effort. But we humans must provide *conditions* favorable to growth: in the case of plants, these are sunshine, water, and good soil; in the case of spiritual beings, these are moral principles, meaningful work, study, and socialization. The latter takes place in both work and home environments and involves communication, sharing, trust, and love.

Jesus' parable highlights the fact that growth proceeds from stage to stage, as does the growth of plants. He seems to be indicating that spiritual growth also proceeds from one level of maturity to another, a notion that shows up in 2 Pet 1:5–8 (knowledge and goodness increasing), but even more clearly in Paul: we are "being transformed . . . from one degree of glory to another," being renewed daily (2 Cor 3:18; 4:16); growing from a child's reasoning to mature reasoning, eventually to "know fully" (1 Cor 13:11–12); "that your love may overflow more and more" (Phil 1:9). The growth principle is foundational to Jesus' own teachings: we are fruit-bearing trees; we are branches that cannot bear fruit unless we remain connected to the vine (Luke 6:43–44; John 15:4–8). A tiny seed grows into a huge bush, taking over the environment like a weed (Mark 4:31–32). This last one highlights the *social* expansion of the movement of believers, but it also has implications for what happens to an individual's seed-faith. In Luke, the mustard seed parable is followed by the parable of a little leaven penetrating the whole dough (13:21), illustrating a connection between the faith of a few individuals (a few sprinkles of leaven) and the effect on society (the whole lump is leavened).

The "stalk to head to fruit" parable also draws out the fact that each evolutionary stage prophesies the next. The early church's "rule of faith" affirmed that the OT testified to the Messiah. The notion seems to be that each phase of revelation anticipates the next phase. The NT looks beyond itself to a messianic age, a new phase of religious development where loyalty is voluntary, freedom is handled with maturity, and we all grow up into the full measure of Christ. It is not just faith, but *character* that matters: we bear "fruit" (actions) arising from our state of spiritual health: the "good tree bears good fruit, but the bad tree bears bad fruit. . . . Either make the tree good, and its fruit good; or make the tree bad, and its fruit bad" (Matt 7:17; 12:33; cf. "fruit of the Spirit" in Gal 5:22).

The family metaphor entails growth, and this is confirmed by the Lord's repeated usage of images of farming, sowing, plant-growing, fruit-bearing, and leaven-rising. Growth and fruit-bearing are principles of the spiritual life, as of the organic life, and Jesus draws attention to this, though mainly with imagery rather than explanation. He seems to assume that, as people grow spiritually, they will bear spiritual fruits and will recognize the growth pattern. But he does nudge them toward such recognition. If we do not bear fruits within a reasonable time, we will be cut down, just as a barren tree that does not respond to agricultural care will eventually be cut down (Luke 13:6–9).

The *necessity* of growth is the message behind some of Jesus' apparently harsh sayings, for instance the parable of the pounds or talents, wherein a nobleman expects each of his servants to invest the talents he has been given and to be able to show some kind of profit, however small, and is angry with the servant who buried his talent and did not make any profit from it. This servant is not condemned for having been given only one talent but for not making any profit upon it. "Profit," of course, is metaphoric for "spiritual growth and progress." The nobleman's anger with the unprofitable servant seems harsh unless one grasps the parable's main point: one needs to "invest" one's God-given talents so that they grow and gain "profit." Jesus does not just *wish* for spiritual growth, he *insists* on it.

There is a growth imperative—grow, or you will lose what has been given to you. This is what is meant by "to all those who have, more will be given, and they will have an abundance; but from those who have nothing, even what they have will be taken away" (Matt 25:29).[1] As we see from what precedes it, this means: more responsibility will be given to those who show they can reap a spiritual profit, while those who are not making *any* spiritual gains are in danger of losing even the spiritual endowment they have. People are not expected to make an impossible profit. Note this! The two-talent servant who made two talents of profit receives exactly the same praise as the five-talent servant who made five talents of profit (Matt 25:20–23). Luke misses this point completely, changing the parable by having everyone receiving ten talents in the beginning (19:13). This is not true to life. As Matthew recognizes, talents are unequally given to people, "to each according to his ability" (Matt 25:15). Luke has somewhat of an obsession with equality, and it ironically leads him to make the nobleman in the parable harsh and violently judgmental (19:27). In fact, equalitarianism *is* harsh, when it does not recognize that people are differently endowed. My point is not to favor Matthew over Luke, for there are other parables where Matthew's Israel-obsession seems to get in the way, while the broad-minded Luke gets the point. Matthew and Luke received different talents!

Believers receive many benefits (even new talents) by recognizing the truth of the growth imperative. We are able to appreciate the hard-won

---

1. Mark does not have the parable of the talents but has the "taken away" saying (4:25), understanding it to mean "the measure you give will be the measure you get, and still more will be given you" (4:24). This shows the abundance of spiritual growth, as does the bearing of "fruit, thirty and sixty and a hundredfold" (4:20).

victories of the spirit, noting the limitations of time in which they occurred, and the strength of the opposition that was overcome. We learn to appreciate our heritage of the spirit and to not despise our ancestors for their level of culture, any more than we would despise children for their undeveloped thinking.

Growth studies is a relatively neglected area of theology, except in connection with developmental psychology. The most important psychological studies have been those of Lawrence Kohlberg[2] and Erik Erikson.[3] Of course, their theories stand in need of revision.[4] The most interesting theological reflections on psychological models, those of James Fowler[5] and Donald Capps,[6] are not overly dependent upon any single author.

One of the richest areas of current thought is this focus on the spiritual side of psychosocial growth, because it adds scientific advancement to spiritual progress. In fact, there is a progress imperative, even a spiritualization imperative, that operates upon and *moves* the spiritual life of humanity, an influence from God within our mentality that insists: "*grow!*" — "Be perfect, therefore, as your heavenly Father is perfect" (Matt 5:48). Of course, it will take forever to even approach a fulfillment of this command . . . but we *have* forever!

Fowler looks at numerous scholars who have proposed models for interpreting development by stages. The three most important are probably Piaget, who studied the degrees of cognitive development; Kohlberg, who mapped out stages of moral development; and Erikson, who strove to integrate psychological and social-functional development. Faith development is to be distinguished from these other models. There will be substantial overlap, but faith has its own unique concerns, such as developing a concept of spiritual powers and presences, discerning spiritual values, trusting divine guidance, and finding ways to cope with suffering and evil.

2. Kohlberg, *Philosophy of Moral Development*.

3. Erikson, *Childhood and Society*; idem, *Toys and Reasons*; idem, *Identity and the Life Cycle*; idem, *The Life Cycle Completed*.

4. Gilligan says that Kohlberg highlights the keys to *male* moral development (rules, rights, and justice), which makes the female focus on relationships "appear to be deficient in moral development" (Gilligan, *Different Voice*, 18). But I think that there is more overlap than Gilligan admits. She identifies "responsibility" as key to female moral development (ibid., 21, 65), but it is equally central in male moral development. The "rules" are all about responsibility.

5. Fowler, *Stages of Faith*.

6. Capps, *Life Cycle Theory and Pastoral Care*; idem, "Decades of Life."

There are considerable corollaries between Erikson's phases and Fowler's. Fowler reshapes of the last four of Erikson's stages, asserting that the basic conflict faced by people of ages 13 to 20 is between identity cohesion and identity confusion; the conflict from roughly 21 to 34 is intimacy vs. isolation; the conflict from ages 35 to 59 it is generativity vs. stagnation; and from 60 onwards it is integrity vs. despair.[7] Fowler explores the role of faith in peoples' attempts to negotiate each of these challenges, as well as drawing out the age ranges at which these stages are generally traversed. Donald Capps also finds that Erikson had clustered too many of the stages early in life (four of the eight are in childhood), and he re-positions the eight stages to cover eight decades of life.[8] This helps bring out the development of a mature personality. A successful navigation of stage five (identity cohesion) involves "fidelity to values and ideologies."[9] Stage six is where we must either learn to develop intimacy or withdraw into isolation; Erikson had located this in young adulthood; Capps allows that intimacy issues *were* faced in one's twenties, but places the center of this stage in one's fifties, when genital intimacy is no longer of primary importance. Earlier stages do anticipate the issues of later stages. Erikson seems to focus on when the various life issues first emerge, so his stages occur early in life; Capps places them later because he is focusing on the time when each issue becomes of *central* importance.

Stage seven offers one either generativity or stagnation; it can easily be either the most productive or the least productive phase of a person's life. One can be highly productive even if one has experienced some difficulty in the development either of values or of relationships. Some novelists, for instance, are highly productive at this stage of life, but their works suggest a chaotic and meaningless world. These people have failed to develop a healthy value system. Other authors present a useful value system but find themselves alone in their personal lives or with troubled relationships. If the person can find a way to balance and interpret these areas of life, he or she is more prepared to navigate stage eight, where the positive pole is personal integration, and the negative pole is disintegration and despair.

People around the world face similar issues as they move through life. There is a remarkable similarity in the issues faced by the characters in literature from around the world, issues of loneliness, love, industry,

7. Fowler, *Stages of Faith*, 108.
8. Capps, "The Decades of Life," 3–32.
9. Parker and Tate, "Using Erikson's Developmental Theory," 223.

responsibility, perseverance, service, and memories—the cherishing, enduring, and reinterpreting of memories. These are the contents of life as we move from phase to phase, intellectually, socially, and spiritually.

Erikson's system offers considerable hope; "we go through all the stages on schedule"; progress can be difficult, or we can make "good progress," but we *will* go through these stages.[10] For instance, the achievements of stages one and two are "basic trust" and "autonomy," respectively. We can make "accelerated progression from basic trust" to autonomy, or we can "linger excessively over basic trust" (experiencing more mistrust than trust) before moving to autonomy.[11] We will not do Erikson justice in this book. We will instead attempt to do some justice to Fowler's system, which is a little easier to comprehend (having six instead of eight stages) and is, furthermore, focused on faith.

Fowler's Stages of Faith Development

Fowler tries to formulate his system to allow it to apply to any religion or culture. Stage 1 is experienced by children, and he labels it "intuitive-projective," but he could just as well call it "imaginative," since "imaginative processes . . . are unrestrained . . . . productive of longlasting images and feelings (positive and negative)."[12]

Stage 2, "mythic-literal," witnesses the emergence of logic, concepts of reciprocity, and the use of stories to convey meaning; there is an increased interest in realistic stories and a heightened ability "to construct the perspectives of others."[13] This stage manifests enhanced moral reflection, though necessarily in a somewhat dogmatic or dualistic way. "Beliefs are appropriated with literal interpretations, as are moral rules" and symbols are "one-dimensional."[14] Still, this is real moral development. *Fairness* and *conscience* were of central importance to the nine- to eleven-year-olds whom Fowler interviewed.[15] These become more focalized on the next level.

Adolescents generally live at Stage 3, "synthetic-conventional," wherein ideal concepts and propositions become dominant, which can lead to

10. Capps, *Life Cycle Theory*, 19.

11. Ibid.

12. Fowler, *Stages of Faith*, 133.

13. Ibid., 136–37, 139.

14. Ibid., 149.

15. Ibid., 144–46.

harshly judgmental opinions of people and institutions who do not conform to the perceived principles. Conformity is highly valued. Close friendships become very important for confirming self-image. Parallel to this is the valuing of God's support and affirmation of the self.[16] Even though this is normally an adolescent stage, many adults never progress beyond this, the stage of conventional, shared beliefs.[17] Atheists usually get stuck on this level of conventional (anti-)religious views, proudly rejecting the shallow stereotypes they have about religious people and religious ideas.

Stage 4 involves reflection, a questioning of shared value systems, and "a relocation of authority within the self."[18] At this stage of "individuative-reflective faith," things previously considered sacred are now "interrogated by Stage 4's critical questioning," and this can result in "a sense of loss, dislocation, grief." To replace the naivety of the old belief, one must differentiate one's identity and worldview from others and develop "an explicit system of meanings."[19]

Stage 5 leads one into complexity. The intellectual certainty of Stage 4 breaks down; there is a loss of control; paradox and contradiction continue to defeat expectations; and certainty erodes when one begins to see all sides of an issue. Advantages to this stage ("conjunctive faith") are that one learns to accept a certain degree of powerlessness and is more able to recognize the relativity and partiality of one's own understanding; one has experienced "the sacrament of defeat"![20] One has to integrate the "paradoxical dimensions of spirituality" into one's experience, since one's "spiritual grandiosity has been deconstructed."[21] Further, one learns to become more open to others and to encounters with other religious traditions.

The highest stage is "universalizing faith," Stage 6. One is no longer restricted by localized or tribal loyalties, or attached to public acclaim or outward success. The person at Stage 6 often frightens others with his willingness to confront group hypocrisy with "the imperatives of absolute love and justice," without any concern for "threats to the self" or "to the institutional arrangements of the present order." The Stage 6 person realizes

16. Ibid., 152–54, 156.

17. Ibid., 161, 172.

18. Ibid., 179.

19. Ibid., 180, 182.

20. Ibid., 186–87, 198.

21. Sandage and Shults, *Transforming Spirituality*, 234, 237. This part of the book is Sandage's.

that the reality of God and the possibilities of the reign of God exceed all his concepts about them.[22] Stages 5 and 6, then, show a certain humility that is usually lacking in Stages 3 and 4.

It is evident that we can go beyond developmental psychology and begin to study *developmental spirituality*, and we find that Fowler is a pioneer in this field. The systems of Kohlberg or Erikson, of course, have spiritual implications from beginning to end, but Fowler has drawn out faith as a primary theme in human development, and pointed out some inadequacies in the previous theories.

Stages of Religious Conceptualization

I would like to add a more focused scheme of stages religious development, which can complement Fowler's scheme. By saying "more focused," I am not criticizing Fowler, but pointing out that my model is narrowly focused on a specific aspect of faith development, namely the *conceptualizing* of spiritual forces and of God. It is a focus on concepts, beliefs. An advancing concept of God is related to—almost synonymous with—an advancing understanding of the moral reliability of spiritual forces. Thus, my scheme has implications for moral and social progress, but it is not synonymous with social development. Nor is conceptual development identical with personal spiritual progress, though there are parallels. The more immediate parallel to my conceptualization scale is evolution in social religious practices, rituals, and doctrines. The stages proposed by Fowler, Erikson, and Kohlberg encompass more than my scheme does. In order to look at the moral and mental development of the whole person, they were compelled to downplay the issue of religious doctrines. My model zeroes in on the conceptualization of spiritual forces (God, gods, spirits, the Absolute), and complements their models at several points. Comparing different developmental models can help us to understand how people make more progress in one area of their lives than in others, to notice imbalanced development, and perhaps to learn what is needed for overall spiritual growth.

The basics of my four-stage religious conceptualization scheme are fairly simple. Religious thinking begins with a pre-moral stage, dominated by belief in spirits, ghosts, capricious gods, good and bad luck, and magic. The spirit world is perceived as being full of power but not always having clear purpose. The spirits are dangerous and moody.

22. Fowler, *Stages of Faith*, 200, 210.

This gives way to the ritual stage of religion, which emerges when people begin to perceive that the universe is *ordered*. This is the semi-moral stage of religious development; orderliness has moral implications, but it takes a long time for these to mature. Ritual-dominated religion reflects instincts about some degree of order in the spiritual realm, but it also reflects primitive beliefs about the possibility of *manipulating* that order, *persuading* those gods, *mollifying* those ghosts. Yet this stage brings the important recognition that actions have consequences. This carries the seed of moral development, even if it is mainly conceived of magically (the zapping of the fellow who accidentally touched the ark of the covenant; 2 Sam 6:6–7). The concept of sin at this level is more naturalistic than moral (sin can be transferred to a goat, for instance; Lev 16:21–22), but moral consciousness has been born, and it will grow. Sin is a concept with a future. There is an interesting correlation with Kohlberg's system here; my stage two contains both the selfishness of his second stage and the conventional morality of his third stage.

My third level could be called the moral stage, and I can use Leviticus to illustrate this level as well: "You shall not take vengeance or bear a grudge against any of your people, but you shall love your neighbor as yourself" (Lev 19:18). Here it is discerned that God cannot be manipulated, that there is a judgment facing all humans, and that there is a severe separation between good and evil. This level is clearly articulated by the Hebrew prophets and by the great prophet of Iran, Zarathushtra,[23] but it also underlies the viewpoint of the Confucian scriptures and of the earliest Buddhist writing, the *Dhammapada*. Levels two and three share the concept that sin has fatal consequences for the sinner. On level two this is semi-magical and semi-moral, but on level three it is moral: God will judge each person on the basis of his or her moral conduct.

The principle of divine judgment is a key concept on level three, and it has been most fully developed (in fact overdeveloped) in the great monotheistic religions, which have often gotten stuck on this stage, despite scriptural statements against judging others. This stage produces many severe and judgmental statements and conceives of the afterlife as a place of reward and punishment. Judgmental religious force tends to issue either in severe judgment of others or in severe self-judgment, which is very damaging to them. Thus can a very moral religion, when it fails to make

---

23. Scholars now prefer this spelling, with an "sh" instead of an "s" in the last consonant cluster.

progress, drive many of its adherents to abandon the faith. This third level of religious conceptualization matches, in many ways, the conventional and group dominated faith of Fowler's third stage, but it also can match the individualistic but controlling attitude of his fourth stage. "Critical thinkers" are just as prone to being ideologically stuck as are conventional believers.

Entry to the fourth level in my system may require entry into Fowler's fifth level, with its humbling of intellectual conceit, its "sacrament of defeat." Religious ideas remain strong on my fourth level, but they manifest more flexibility and teachability, gained through experience. The values stressed are mercy, love, and the work of spiritual perfecting: "I came not to judge the world, but to save the world" (John 12:47). Concepts are put in service to values. The afterlife is conceived as a place of growth, rather than reward and punishment. "You . . . may become participants of the divine nature" (2 Pet 1:4); "being transformed . . . from one degree of glory to another" (2 Cor 3:18).

The morality that emerges at stage three matures in stage four into a recognition that universally true principles transcend one's level of understanding, but that one's partial understanding is nevertheless worthwhile. One's convictions are strong but not "dogmatic."

My stage four correlates with Kohlberg's sixth stage. True and universal principles reign in Kohlberg's stage six, working for the good of both the individual and the group, though transcending the self-interest of both.[24] Here Kohlberg's "principles" and Gilligan's "interconnectedness" converge.

Sanity, Joy, and Fearlessness

Understanding spiritual growth through stages helps us to better understand human psychology, to more quickly recognize narcissism and bigotry in religious leaders and in the followers who anoint them—but also to recognize that most of the problems we observe are either growing pains or are characteristic of growth delayed: being stuck at a certain stage. When we understand people's values and their struggles, we will feel compassion for them regarding their defects and difficulties, at least for those who have some loyalty to their understanding of God. And if we are of the type that is inclined toward strong self-criticism or self-effacement, we should apply the same compassion to ourselves.

24. Kohlberg, *Philosophy of Moral Development*, 342–47, 409–12.

Some of Jesus' sayings are like sanity tests. Will we be overly literal (and therefore self-destructive) in implementing the command to cut off our hand if it offends us (Matt 5:30), or will we grasp his use of metaphors, *get the main point*, and not get stuck in literalism? Will we have some common sense and proportion in enacting the command "Be perfect, therefore, as your heavenly Father is perfect" (Matt 5:48), which requires eternity for fulfillment, or will we think this needs to be immediately implemented, thus either feeling guilty for not fulfilling it or becoming megalomaniacal and claiming to have fulfilled it? Will we trust that "God . . . gives the growth" (1 Cor 3:7; cf. Mark 4:27; Isa 61:11) or will we become anxious about our pace of growth? Anxiety declines as trust increases, but besides accepting this principle, believers are greatly helped by developing certain techniques, such as the "capacity to self-soothe anxiety and [to] self-validate."[25] These prevent one from becoming angry or judgmental about the fact that one has anxiety.

Jesus made joy and fearlessness a centerpiece of his teaching.[26] Joy is an essential condition for spiritual receptivity. When feeling wounded and abandoned, we may be tempted to think that God is withholding his love from us, but in fact there are certain qualities and blessings that simply cannot be given to anything but a joyous receptor. It is dangerous to give certain things to an angry mind, and it is impossible to give certain things to a despairing heart. But when we make it through our sorrowful places and reach the heights of worship once again, then do we raise our joy-receptors, and God is able to reach us—or we are able to *recognize* God's reaching-out, which had been there all along. Joy and faith are the antidotes to fear.

The psychology of fear underlies many manifestations of religion, such as the manipulative practices of sacrifice, obeisance, rote praise, dramatized acts of self-punishment and self-denial, and other religious gestures designed to change the Deity's attitude (and often to get attention, socially). These behaviors are completely unnecessary, according to Jesus.[27] He taught his disciples to abandon fear and to trust God. The way to God is already open, and nothing needs to be done to persuade the Father: "Do not be afraid, little flock, for it is your Father's good pleasure to give you

25. Sandage and Shults, *Transforming Spirituality*, 180.

26. There is delight in discovering God's love (Matt 13:44; Luke 15:7). Fear is the opposite of faith (Mark 5:36; John 15:9–11). One can rejoice even in the face of suffering (Luke 6:21–23; John 16:20–24).

27. "Whenever you give alms, do not sound a trumpet before you, as the hypocrites do . . . do not heap up empty phrases" (Matt 6:2, 7).

the kingdom"; "Your heavenly Father knows [w]hat you need"; "The Father himself loves you" (Luke 12:32; Matt 6:32; John 16:27).

Trusting God and Jesus enables one to draw on God's and Jesus' healing power. "Your faith has made you well"—The woman who dared to touch his cloak was healed; the blind man who boldly asked for healing received it; the centurion whose faith amazed Jesus, went home to find his servant healed (Matt 9:20–22; Mark 10:46–52; Luke 7:6–10; 18:42). The key to receiving is sincerely asking; God is even more loving than an earthly father, who would not give a snake to his child who had asked for a fish (Luke 11:9–13). Jesus unhesitatingly trusted God. Even though the mature Jesus could read people like a book, knowing their selfishness and deceit, he retained a childlike trust of God, and recommended this attitude to his followers.

When once we really incorporate this attitude, we cease to fear God or to think that we need to persuade God to "have mercy" or to "look kindly upon us." Jesus recommends real trusting, not pious posturing. He does not deny that the afflictions of real life—disease, injury, deformities, natural disasters, poverty, injustice—will continue, and he understands that we still cry out for salvation. But we no longer need to think that these things are the personal visitations of a punishing God. Our prayer life no longer needs to take on the subtly manipulative tone that grows out of anxiety. We can certainly pray, and even supplicate, but we benefit by knowing that God is not personally visiting misfortune upon us. Further, God goes with us through every experience: "In all their affliction he was afflicted" (Isa 63:9 RSV). Thus we learn to pray less for material results and more for intimacy with God and insight into human relationships, as well as help with those relationships. We seek interpersonal values more than personal benefit. We pray more to "our Father" and less to "my God."

Jesus grew up with a healthy-minded religion and had no need of a conversion experience. Those of us who grew up with psychopathology are the ones who have to undergo drastic and wrenching conversion experiences that undo some of our fear-based coping mechanisms and instill hope where fear had lived.[28] We soon learn that some of our injurious mental patterns persist and that healing is a life-long project. Learning to be

---

28. William James is the one who made this distinction between healthy-minded religion and the religion of more troubled souls who have to go through conversion experiences.

re-parented by God is like learning a new language. It takes persistence and repetition of the spiritual decision.

Philosophies of Hope and Despair

What are the stages of development of whole societies? One that is relatively easy to observe is the expansion of polity from the levels of clan to tribe, to confederation of tribes, to national state, to multinational states, to continent-wide polities like the US and supergovernments like the European Community, and perhaps eventually to a world body that is able to replace war and lawlessness with legal arbitration.

But what are the spiritual implications of human development and social evolution? Is there a divine plan? The often overlooked social thinker, Max Scheler, spoke of "three supreme purposes of growth which knowledge . . . serve[s]." First there is "knowledge of control or achievement," which has to do with science and technology. This "leads us to the next higher purpose, 'knowledge of culture,'" which brings personal growth while yet involving knowledge of the whole world. Finally there is "knowledge of salvation or of grace," in which we participate in the source of life while "the ultimate source itself" participates more fully in created things, "'knows' itself and the world, in us and through us, *itself* attains its timeless aim of growth."[29] Thus do we help God to achieve God's own intention to grow into the world. (The eternal God does not grow, but the divine purpose active in the world *does* grow.) God is both transcendent (traditional theology) and immanent (process theology).

The last eighty years have witnessed a serious loss of faith in the transformative possibilities of science and ethical religion working together for the enlightenment of the human race, for rational discourse to replace war, and understanding to replace religious bigotry. Many disillusioned, dispirited, and confused people today have little concept of human evolution having any spiritual goal. Today, the confidence of previous generations, that "the Eternal Spirit can help the human spirit to conquer or to find a way around every unspiritual obstacle"[30]—seems like an illusion. What was written fifty years ago seems incomprehensible: that Christ is the "omega point" of human evolution, radiating "the energies which lead the universe

29. Scheler, "Forms of Knowledge and Culture," 42–43. Spinoza and Hegel had such theories (43).

30. Brightman, *The Spiritual Life*, 174.

back to God through his humanity,"[31] the idea of a "descending . . . Christogenesis" and "an ascending anthropogenesis."[32]

Such enthusiasm about a Christic transformation of the human race is alien to our current state of disappointment about human progress. All such hopes are labeled "naive" or "imperialist" by "progressive" academics who sneer at the idea of a divine plan for spiritual progress. The common accusation that Teilhard was naive about evil is not entirely fair; the middle portion of *The Divine Milieu*, for instance, concerns "our struggle with God against evil," the "duty to resist evil," and "the setbacks caused by [creation's] moral downfalls."[33]

Meanwhile, ordinary people are either losing hold of traditional beliefs or seizing onto them with fanatical and panicky zeal. There is an eerie parallelism between those who want to return to an imagined religious correctness of the past while seeking to suppress religious questioning, and those who repudiate all faiths of the past and seek to suppress those who actually believe in something. There is an ironic similarity between fundamentalism and nihilism, one using simplistic dogmatic answers to eliminate all uncertainty, the other using dogmatic uncertainty to eliminate all answers. One aspires to hyper-Biblicism, the other to hyper-criticism. There is considerable pretense in both postures. Both have lost connection with the real-time activity of God within the human mind, and so resort to a *system* to answer all questions (or to question all answers).

Postmodernism

I had planned this section to be an attack on postmodernism, but I continue to encounter theists who call themselves postmodernists, so I must specify that I am attacking *atheistic* postmodernism, which is nothing but nihilism learning new tricks. It is a return of skepticism, the weakest of the four major philosophies of the Hellenistic age.[34] Nihilism makes an absolute out of the notion that there are no absolutes; it is certain that there is

31. Teilhard de Chardin, *The Divine Milieu*, 123.

32. Teilhard de Chardin, *Human Energy*, 179.

33. Teilhard de Chardin, *Divine Milieu*, 83, 91, and 104, respectively.

34. Stoicism was the strongest, having considerable interest in the Divine, as did its predecessor Cynicism, though the latter was antisocial to an impractical degree. Even Epicureanism had some value, having strong scientific leanings. These three took ethics seriously.

no certainty. Why, then would a theist want to utilize this philosophy? One postmodern theist claims that it helps to de-throne self-deifying pride of either the religious or intellectualizing type,[35] and that this useful aspect is "not conceptually tied to the atheistic part."[36] In other words, relativism is *relatively* useful. This means that only one rather unremarkable aspect of postmodernism is of any use, the rather obvious insight that human understanding is shaped by culture, and limited by finitude of intellect. One hardly needs the baggage of "postmodernism" to make such a point.

Westphal utilizes postmodernism, but his religiously useful ideas come from traditional theology; he has to use revelation[37] and future eschatology[38] to escape from the despair implicit in postmodernism. Westphal's point that human understanding is limited is valid but unremarkable, and need not be linked to a philosophy that leans toward atheism and treats the subject of truth as a joke. Theists do not need to feel any debt to this trend. Theists need no help from postmodernism to study the limitations of human understandings of truth and of God.

I offer a similar caution to theists who would affirm deconstructionism, one of the ancestors of postmodernism. René Girard says that deconstructionists are actually very Christian ("against Christianity of course") in their impulse to defend society's victims, although "the defence of the victim entails new persecutions!"[39] Girard points out that it was the Christian revelation that took the side of victims and opposed the violent scapegoating of the majority.[40] I would agree that, despite the fading of religious belief, many people inherit their ethical instincts from Christianity, but I would point out that hostility to theism undermines the ethical impulse, making people susceptible to false ideologies and to "politically correct" forms of blaming and scapegoating. As Girard mourns, "One can persecute today only in the name of being against persecution."[41] Ethics of an unconsciously Christian origin cannot thrive without faith in God. Without

---

35. Westphal, *Overcoming Onto-Theology*, 155–56. "Self-deifying" is on 156.

36. Ibid., 173.

37. Ibid., 174.

38. Ibid., 204.

39. Girard, *Evolution and Conversion*, 258.

40. His early book, *Things Hidden Since the Foundation of the World*, is the most vivid in spelling out his theory of the Christian exposé of the violent mechanism of selecting and killing human scapegoats.

41. Girard, *Evolution and Conversion*, 258.

God and a belief in the afterlife, there is no morality, as Dostoyevsky said.[42] Ethics without God is like music without melody, a person without a soul. Many well-intentioned secularists are experiencing a failed form of transition from stage three (conformist religion) to stage four (reflective, personally responsible religion). They reflect, they try to be responsible, but they have lost hold of the lifeline. They have let go of conformist religion but also of faith in *any* transcendent reality, and so of any real hope for humanity or for themselves.

In a chapter on the stages of growth, it was necessary to mention some of the retrograde ideologies that stifle growth. There simply is no progress without courageous venture beyond dogmatism, without honest wrestling with life's challenges. Responsible living always entails uncertainty and struggle, but one can remain certain of the abiding presence of God, who is not in a hurry, who has all of eternity to "bring to completion"—to *perfect*—the work he began in each one of us (Phil 1:6).

Spiritual courage and endurance are necessary character traits for anyone who would make spiritual progress. We must avoid falling into comfortable ideologies that shut off honest discussion. If we can embrace the struggle, uncertainty, and decision-making that are essential for growth, we may gain confidence that "It is God who is at work in you" (Phil 2:13). This is what Tillich refers to as "the courage to be," a quality of spiritual intentionality that enables us to keep our spiritual focus even in the face of intense anxieties.[43]

---

42. "Destroy a man's belief in immortality and . . . nothing would be immoral then, everything would be permitted . . . crime must not only be tolerated but even recognized . . . There is no virtue if there is no immortality" (Dostoyevsky, *The Brothers Karamazov*, 80 [book 2, chap. 6]).

43. Tillich, *The Courage to Be*, 81–85.

THREE

"Do not despise one of these little ones"
Welcoming the Child

THE GOSPEL SUGGESTS CERTAIN connections between God, our concept of humanity, and practical theology. Jesus' gospel pictures human *familiarity* to God—that is, a family relationship to a God who is accessible. If we accept this, then we must correlate theology and anthropology instead of setting them against each other with a despairing doctrine of humanity as depraved and hopelessly disconnected from God. Hyper-pessimistic theology suppresses the kindness of God, denies the divinity within people, and leads to a dread of God, to wrong-headed ideas about children, and to pathological parenting. Fear of an angry God leads to the notion that most of us will be sent to a place of unceasing torment, which will be eternal misery for us, but eternal revenge for God. Thus did we remake the Father of Jesus into this image of God as a vengeful (and insecure) tyrant.

Our religious ideas are infected with our own psychopathology, itself originating in dysfunctional families. But the teaching of Jesus that God is an infinitely caring father (not an insecure, controlling one) leads instead to a healthy family dynamic, and to a concept of the afterlife as a place of continued growth within the divine family.

Religious teaching deeply affects family ethics and thus the psychological condition of the people who grow up in such families. Religion, ethics, psychology, and family life have mutual and reciprocal effects. Fear-based religious ideas only ring true for people who grew up in a fear-based atmosphere, while children who grew up with loving and communicative parents will not find it difficult to believe in an accessible and loving Divine Parent. A healthy parental pair models divinity more effectively than does a resentful and embittered parental pair. Thus does the home life shape religious intuitions, yet also religious concepts can change the mood and behavior within the home. We are not hopelessly trapped in a psychology derived from our home life. We *can* become reoriented by truth and experience a changed dynamic in our thinking and living. "Get yourselves a new heart and a new spirit!" (Ezek 18:31). "Turn to me and be saved!" (Isa 45:22).

As long as we approach God with a prisoner's mentality, we will approach family life in the same way, with ideologies of punishment and domination, and our families will become laboratories for our psychopathology. But if we learn to stop living by fear, stop conceiving of salvation as magical rescue from doom, then we can begin to understand that we are members of God's family, and that salvation is about *life* rather than escape or ransom. The Divine Parent gives life, provides a plan for guidance and growth, and restores vitality and personal warmth whenever they have been damaged (or we *perceive* them to have been damaged). When we see that salvation is about life, growth, and the inculcation of Godly character, we will stop using religion for magic and manipulation. Family values without psychopathology become possible.

The Qualities of a Child

Jesus links membership in the kingdom with childlike honesty and humility; it is these *qualities* of a child that enable adults to enter into the life that Jesus brings: "Unless you change and become like children, you will never enter the kingdom of heaven. Whoever becomes humble like this child is the greatest in the kingdom of heaven" (Matt 18:3–4). It *does* take humility for an adult to become a child—that is, to admit neediness and to become teachable. It is this teachability that Jesus seems to have in view in all four gospels. It may be that Mark and Luke stress the child's openness to receiving a gift, while Matthew puts "a particular emphasis on humility,"[1] but all four gospels speak, in their own ways, of receiving the kingdom of God *as* a child (Matt 18:3; Mark 10:15; Luke 18:17; John 1:12; 3:3).

Not only does this teaching exalt certain qualities of honesty and humility, it asks believers to show respect for actual children. "Let the little children come to me" (Matt 19:15). He answers the question "who is the greatest in the kingdom?" by calling a child to him, and putting the child "among them" (Matt 18:1–2), but the child is not just a metaphor. Jesus

1. Francis, "Children and Childhood in the New Testament," 76–77.

concretely warns against putting "a stumbling block before one of these little ones" and against "despis[ing] one of these little ones" (18:6, 10). He draws attention to the vulnerability and value of children.

When his disciples try to send away children who wanted to come to him, he rebukes them, and uses this occasion for a teaching lesson in gospel basics:

> He was indignant and said to them, "Let the little children come to me; do not stop them; for it is to such as these that the kingdom of God belongs. Truly I tell you, whoever does not receive the kingdom of God as a little child will never enter it" (Mark 10:14–15).

In fact, Jesus creates the basis for the enlightened treatment of children, using the child as a symbol or "envoy of the Kingdom,"[2] and defending the dignity of actual children. Jesus makes *acceptance* of the child equivalent to accepting himself: "Whoever welcomes one such child in my name welcomes me" (Matt 18:5). Jesus may be "granting children almost divine status" here.[3] At the very least he is saying that they can "receive what is *properly theirs*—the reign of God."[4] This was unprecedented. Not even the Greco-Roman sages placed such importance on children, as Jesus did.[5] In fact, Jesus was challenging the prevailing Greco-Roman concepts of fatherhood and authority by calling God a forgiving "father" who accepted the outcast. His use of "father" for God is "a subversive act" that "challenges traditional ideas about male authority."[6]

Jesus makes it clear that one can hardly do the right thing religiously unless one changes one's attitude toward children. The two realms are no longer separable. If you do real damage to a child ("put a stumbling block before one of these little ones") you have committed an atrocity, and "it would be better for you if a great millstone were fastened around your neck and you were drowned in the depth of the sea" (Matt 18:6). Rather than asserting fatherly rights over the child, Jesus articulates the new and more civilized view that parenting is more a matter of responsibility than of rights.

---

2. Ibid., 73.

3. Miller-McLemore, *Let the Children Come*, 97.

4. Gundry-Volf, "The Least and the Greatest," 60.

5. Westfall, "Family in the Gospels and Acts," 128.

6. Rubio, *Christian Theology of Marriage*, 140.

Mark tells us "he was indignant" with the apostles for trying to keep the children away from him: "do not stop them; for it is to such as these that the kingdom of God belongs"; and he dramatized his attitude when "he took them up in his arms, laid his hands on them, and blessed them" (Mark 10:14, 16; cf. Luke 18:15–17; Matt 19:13–15). Exclusion of children from the presence of Jesus is contrary to the gospel. Further, the failure to achieve childlike honesty and trust is fatal to one's *own* approach to God.

The very qualities of the child that Jesus exalts are the ones that enable healthy socialization and prevent narcissism. The honesty of the child opens up channels of communication and relationship from humans to angels to God: "in heaven their angels continually see the face of my Father in heaven" (Matt 18:10). This raises the concept of children's spirituality.[7] When adults overcome the fear that leads them to take themselves hyper-seriously, they will recover the ability to talk to God, an ability that comes naturally to children. When children are beaten or neglected, however, they lose the ability to communicate trustfully. Such wounded children, when they become adults, compensate for their anxieties by constructing a façade of toughness or indifference in order to hide their fear, causing them to become dishonest about their own feelings and thus *unable* to communicate honestly.

While the *qualities* of a child (honesty, eagerness) are needed for salvation, and the *image* of the child stands for any believer, the *reality* of particular children becomes the focus of Christian ethics. Parallel with this is the fact of Jesus' close approach to, and compassion for, women, which raised the status of women. Christianity brought significant change in the ethics of family life. Paul makes the radical suggestion that, though the husband rules the wife, *the wife rules the husband* as well (1 Cor 7:4).[8]

Attention to Parenting

Despite Jesus' demonstration of respect for women, and Paul's emphasis on mutual respect within marriage, the Gentile church eventually returned to the patriarchal family structure, with the authoritarianism of the unhappy mother over her children, and of the insecure father over both. But the gospel message refuses to lie dormant, and the initial values are being

7. Miller-McLemore, *Let the Children Come*, 97–98.
8. See Greer, *Broken Lights and Mended Lives*, 100.

rediscovered in our time. More parents are heeding the advice, "Fathers, do not provoke your children, or they may lose heart" (Col 3:21).

The Pauline teachings express some conservatism, but also some radicalism. In them, "parents are to submit to children, though in a different way . . . by not provoking children but treating them with kindness and respect."[9] Gundry-Volf sees the Colossians passage repeating Jesus' idea that children have an "unmediated relationship to the Lord," but children are not held up "as models for adult believers," as they are by Jesus.[10]

Some of the ethical results of Jesus' teaching have only begun to manifest in the later twentieth century and early twenty-first century, paralleled and assisted by advances in developmental and family psychology, and as the ethics of parenting have risen to a place of prominent attention in American culture. Many parents treat their children with considerably more fairness and respect than they were shown when they were children. This added attention is very much *needed* because there are powerful forces that work to erode parents' ability to give children the unhurried time and attention they need: the increased absence of many mothers from the household during the day; a breakdown in neighborhood friendliness; heightened worries about strangers and sexual predators; and a constant temptation toward pleasure seeking and intellectual shallowness. We need to reawaken to the fact that:

> Parenting is a school of dying—dying to self-centered existence and experiencing rebirth in self-giving for the sake of another. Parenting means abandoning control.[11]

Control is precisely what the immature parent fears losing. But American culture is becoming aware of this problem. The increased attention to parenting, psychology, and spirituality is healthy. Popular books are drawing upon the advancing wisdom in the fields of child and adult psychology and parenting. Many people are trying to untangle the knots of blame, resentment, and enmeshment that have suffocated their relationships and made them miserable. Practical theology is contributing to the parenting task, and many parents are more well-equipped to raise children than *their* parents were.

9. Gundry-Volf, "The Least and the Greatest," 57.

10. Ibid., 55–56, 58.

11. Granberg-Michaelson, "Parenting and Reparenting," 31.

Parenting Sanctified

The gradual decline in the concept of a punishing God has been good for family life. If people really believed in a violently angry God who would punish a depraved and worthless humanity for eternity, they would always be violent and severe with their children. They would have to consider their children evil to the bone and schoolable only through beatings. Rational communication would be pointless; *pain* would be the only instructor. Parenting would be nothing but coercion . . . but that is totally opposed to what Jesus is saying, and fortunately, we hear less of that kind of talk today. Abusive parenting and pessimistic anthropology go together, and are fed by degraded religious doctrine.

Am I preparing to make a pronouncement against all conservative parenting styles? No. It is true that "authoritarian views of God are associated with authoritarian childrearing attitudes that encourage strict discipline and make little allowance for opposition to parental authority."[12] Cruel punishment of children does real harm to them. But the key factor in preventing psychological damage to the child seems to be parental motivation, the quality of the parents' spiritual consecration. The key factor in healthy parenting is the degree to which the concept of parenting is "sanctified" as a sacred responsibility, the degree to which discipline is genuinely motivated by love and not by conscious or unconscious vengeful motives in the parents.

Both conservative and liberal parents benefit from considering their parental duty a sanctified calling: "As religiously conservative parents see their role as more sanctified, they may be more likely to interact in positive ways with their children."[13] This increased intimacy was accompanied, among conservative mothers, with *increased* use of corporal punishment, while among mothers with liberal beliefs "greater sanctification of parenting was tied to decreased corporal punishment."[14] Among *both* groups of parents, however, increased concepts of sanctification were accompanied with "decreased rates of parental yelling," increased levels of family warmth,[15] and "with higher levels of parental consistency."[16] This study serves as a

12. Dumas and Nissley-Tsiopinis, "Parental Global Religiousness," 307.

13. Murray-Swank et al., "Sanctification of Parenting," 284.

14. Ibid., 271. More data were collected from mothers than from fathers in this study (285).

15. Ibid., 273.

16. Ibid., 279.

warning against a blanket condemnation of conservative parents, although condemnation of child-beating *is* appropriate.

Together, these studies seem to suggest that the psychological security and trustingness of many "liberal" parents needs to be combined with the religious seriousness that is sometimes more characteristic of "conservative" parents.

More than any particular techniques or ideologies, it is the genuine loyalties and motivations of the parents that determine the quality of their parenting. "What is born of the flesh is flesh, and what is born of the Spirit is spirit" (John 3:6), and the differences are inscribed on children's minds. Spiritual loyalties matter the most. This should not surprise us.

Obviously, some people are thoroughly unprepared for the task of parenting. We currently have complete anarchy in the realm of child-*bearing*, and considerable confusion in the realm of child-*rearing*. Anyone, regardless of maturity or sanity level, is considered to have a God-given right to have children. We really know better than that; we know that highly dysfunctional parents will inflict great suffering on their children and great difficulties on society. Child protective service agencies are caught between the mandate to protect children and the mandate to let birth parents raise their children, at almost any cost. This means that many children remain in abusive homes. Perhaps with time our institutions will evolve more wisdom about how to responsibly handle troubled families. Child protection is a relatively new social science.

Spirituality, Respect

Of course, the solution to abusive parenting is not *neglectful* parenting. Timid parents who are afraid of their children are as stuck in narcissism as bullying parents are. Fear underlies both sets of behavior. The usual cover-up for fear is anger and violence, but sometimes it is paralysis and timidity. Thus, parents need to attend to their own spiritual growth and learn to respond to fear with spiritual intention, courage, faith in God's help, and with wise parental principles. There is a reciprocal beneficial effect between cultivation of spirituality and acceptance of the culture's best learning about enlightened parenting.

Fortunately, many parents work hard to prevent a replication of the cruelty they experienced. The most astounding change in our culture in the last thirty years has nothing to do with computers or cell phones; it is the spiritual and ethical progress in family life, at least among educated people. Sensitivity to the spiritual value of the individual child has been noticeably heightened. Actually this is a continuation of a hundred fifty years of advancing ethics. In 1861, Horace Bushnell's *Christian Nurture* advocated nonviolent methods of dealing with children.[17] When parents "batter and bruise" children, he said, they are "extinguishing in them what they ought to cultivate."[18]

Bushnell rejected the common view of children as inherently sinful, alienated from God, and in need of conversion.[19] Children should be bathed in the love and security of a Christian household, so that the love of God would be an easy notion for them to accept. "You are not to be a savage to them, but a father and Christian. . . . religion is a first thing with you. And it must be first, not in words and talk, but visibly first in your love."[20]

We need not condemn all previous generations when we find that a more advanced insight is available to our generation. Every generation is offered opportunities to advance in some aspect of culture. In our time, advances in ethics and psychology enable us to develop more appropriate ethics of parenting, and enable us to see that "violence against children is harmful."[21]

Children need to be shown respect. Only panicky and insecure parents feel threatened by the respect imperative, which they correctly perceive to be a threat to the ideology of the domination and "punishment" of children.

Families and therapists are learning more about the fact that misbehavior in children is symptomatic of problems in the whole family system. Unfortunately, the instinctive reaction of the parents is to blame the child, who is, in fact, "the most helpless to affect a process that has made them into the family symptom-bearer. . . . Any problem in a child is the result of multigenerational processes."[22] Problems with children are frequently

---

17. Bushnell, *Christian Nurture*. He claimed if people were raised according to Christian principles, they would not need traumatic conversion experiences (cited in Greven, *Spare the Child*, 86). He was against the prevailing doctrine of breaking children's wills (Greven, 87–88).

18. Bushnell, *Christian Nurture*, 44; Greven, *Spare the Child*, 89.

19. Dorrien, *The Making*, 135.

20. Bushnell, *Christian Nurture*, 56–57.

21. Greven, *Spare the Child*, 220–21.

22. Friedman, *Generation to Generation*, 100, 102.

helped when grandparents are involved in the counseling process.[23] Blame is not the issue; healing is.

Generally, the quality of the parental relationship determines the quality of the child-rearing. Spouses who have learned to give and take, to speak and listen, to grow and adapt, make better parents. From the very beginning, Christian thinkers have contemplated the implications of Jesus' gospel and ethics for married life. Perhaps the premier thinker of the "social gospel" movement was Shailer Mathews, who noted that Jesus focused on forgiveness and reconciliation, and his rejection of divorce meant a heightened focus on forgiveness and reconciliation within marriage.[24]

The Equal-Regard Family

In his influential theological study *Agape*, Gene Outka used the terms "equal regard" and "mutuality" to describe a longstanding theme in Christian ethical thought: "One may start with 'regard.' Minimally . . . the neighbor ought to be cared about for his own sake."[25] Love shows reverence, *appreciating* the other, but not seeking to *control* the other.[26] "The other is held to be irreducibly valuable . . . prior to his doing anything in particular which differentiates him from other men."[27]

Don Browning uses these ideas to spearhead his quest for an ethic of the "equal-regard family." First, Browning's effort entails "an equal mother-father team."[28] It involves getting "theologians, philosophers, and social scientists to cooperate in the cultural work of reviving marriage . . . retaining male commitment . . . but uncoupling this commitment from the lingering shadows of patriarchy."[29] It means "treating the other as an end—a child of God," while also expecting to be treated the same way, but not making love *conditional* upon any such reciprocity: "love for the other is not conditioned by the response of the other."[30]

23. Ibid., 106.

24. Mathews, *Jesus on Social Institutions*, 83.

25. Outka, *Agape*, 9.

26. I paraphrase Outka (10), who is quoting H. Richard Niebuhr, *The Purpose of the Church*, 35.

27. Outka, *Agape*, 12.

28. Browning, *Equality and the Family*, 83.

29. Ibid., 307.

30. Browning, "Introduction: The Equal-Regard Family," 7.

One critic of the equal-regard family seems to miss this emphasis on unconditional love, saying that the equal-regard family is overly focused on mutuality and thus on self-interest. Timothy Jackson argues for the traditional Christian focus on *agape*, which stresses self-emptying over mutuality. "*Agape* must precede, restrain, and reform liberty and equality, not merely affirm or translate them."[31] Christ wanted "to reconfigure all temporal human relations, including marriage and parenting, *away from* economies of exchange and personal fulfillment."[32] Jackson's principles are needed, but one must ask whether they have to be expressed as an objection to Browning. It might be more constructive to allow the concept of *agape* to be balanced with Browning's point about mutual respect and psychological health. Jackson stands more in need of correction by Browning, than does Browning by Jackson. Without sane and practical ethics, what seems to be *agape* may really be a narcissistic drive to correct others. The poorly socialized *agapic* person is more provocative and judgmental than helpful or serving. In order to deepen and broaden ethics, which is what *agape* strives to do, it must show some respect for the mutuality that is already in place. The extra-mile effort of *agape* should not demolish the first mile of *mutual* love that exists. If one is perpetually outside the system, one does not help the system but only gets hurt by it. *Agape* should be the intelligent and free choice of a well-rounded person, not the compulsive drive of an imbalanced, though spiritually minded, person. Browning's system contributes to well-roundedness and maturity, and Jackson's *apagic* person needs that maturity in order to be effective.

Browning and his conversation partners seek to fit the equal-regard family into a broader discipline: "Critical familism is . . . the 'theory, practice, and ecology' of . . . the 'committed, intact, equal-regard, public-private family.'"[33] One critic calls critical familism an "attempt to reformulate a Christian understanding of marriage and family in the light of a dominant late liberal ethos," and this is "seen in a steadfast refusal to assign any *inherent* value to sacrificial love."[34] Waters' critique seems overstated. Browning has not rejected any essential ethics or commitment by standing apart from the drama of suffering and self-diminishment that lies behind the rhetoric

31. Jackson, "Judge William and Professor Browning," 145.

32. Ibid., 148.

33. Browning, *Equality and the Family*, 406. The internal quotes are from his *From Culture Wars*, 2.

34. Waters, *Family in Christian Social and Political Thought*, 242.

of "sacrifice." Waters does not notice the occasions when Browning *does* speak of: "sacrificial love (the meaning of the cross) not as an end in itself but as the second mile of enduring love sometimes needed to restore the core of love."[35] Browning is right to be wary of the overemphasis on "sacrifice" in many circles, but he accepts the noble values traditionally associated with the term.

"Sacrifice" is a complex and dual-edged value, which can be used to describe devoted concentration, unselfish giving, or unhealthy and manipulative passive aggressiveness full of blame and revenge. One of the most toxic parental remarks is "I've sacrificed everything for you ungrateful children, and I get nothing in return." Another side of sacrifice, which can be discerned in ritual systems around the world, is the concept of sacrifice as payment, even as purchasing favor from the deity. Plato condemns those who think the gods "are easy to win over when bribed by offerings and prayers," by "offerings and flatteries."[36] Several Hebrew prophets saw manipulation at the heart of the sacrificial cult, and poured scorn upon the idea of the Lord delighting "in the blood of bulls, or of lambs," "burnt offerings," or "ten thousands of rivers of oil" (Isa 1:11; Jer 6:20; Mic 6:7).

Browning seems to be aware of, without deeply examining, the manipulativeness that so often undermines the values of "sacrifice." He treads very cautiously around this problem. He does say "love as equal regard mediates between modern individualism and older ethics of extreme duty and self-sacrifice,"[37] which implies there was something quite wrong about the "older ethics." To do justice to this topic requires sufficient attention both to self-giving (Waters' emphasis) and to ethical and psychological functionality (Browning's emphasis). Waters is really restating Browning's focus when he writes, "the principal purpose of a family is to provide a place of mutual and timely belonging rather than perpetuate a lineage or satisfy parental longings."[38]

Individualism has been a necessary, but destabilizing, factor coming into marriages in the last century or two. Most Americans feel the tension between the traditional idea of "marriage as founded on obligation" and the newer idea of love as the deeply personal "expression of the choices of the

---

35. Browning, *Equality and the Family*, 404.

36. Plato, *Laws* 10.885C; 10.948C.

37. Browning, *Equality and the Family*, 128.

38. Waters, *Family in Christian Social*, 199.

free selves who make it up."[39] "The new atmosphere creates more sensitive, more open, more intense . . . relationships" but also "renders those same relationships fragile and vulnerable."[40]

Browning mentions the work of some writers on the harmful pressures on the modern family,[41] on the value of the intact mother-father unit,[42] and on "an ethic of equal regard" in biblical stories.[43] A number of studies conclude that fathers play a key role in the emotional and cognitive development of children.[44] Psychological research affirms "the importance of an *early* involvement of fathers with their children" and the "father's significant contribution to the emotional well-being of his daughters," as well as sons.[45] Fathers help children learn impulse-control; "evidence points to the father as a modulator of aggressive drive" in children.[46]

Browning comments on the damage the Industrial Revolution did to the father-son relationship. Taking fathers away from the home, industrial work "broke formal and informal initiation rites between fathers and their sons. Women were indeed discriminated against in industrial society, but men may have lost their way entirely."[47]

When fathers lose their way, sons lose their way. When young men lose their way, they become the primary source of crime and violence in society. But young men can also experience a dramatic turnaround in their lives, when they find a new parent in God. Dynamic experience of the love of God is, at first, explosive and transforming, but it commences a process of re-parenting and maturation that takes a lifetime (and beyond). Religious growth and social responsibility go together. A born-again experience can successfully reposition a person in society. But narrow fundamentalist

39. Bellah et al., *Habits of the Heart*, 93, 107.

40. Ibid., 110.

41. Browning, *Equality and the Family*, 92–94, citing Alan Wolfe, *Whose Keeper?*; Lasch, *Haven in a Heartless World*; and Popenoe, *Disturbing the Nest*.

42. For instance Waite and Gallagher, *The Case for Marriage*; Popenoe, *Life without Father*; and Wilson, *On Human Nature*.

43. Browning, *Equality and the Family*, 308, citing Perdue, "The Household, Old Testament Theology," 223–57; Cahill, *Between the Sexes*; and Schüssler Fiorenza, *In Memory of Her*.

44. Browning, *Equality and the Family*, 116, citing Snarey, *How Fathers Care for the Next Generation* and McLanahan, *Growing up with a Single Parent*.

45. Miller, *Calling God "Father,"* 98, 102.

46. Herzog, "On Father Hunger," 172; cf. Miller, *Calling God "Father,"* 97.

47. Browning, *Equality and the Family*, 92.

beliefs make for rigid relationships and judgmental attitudes. Thus, once the religious experience has begun, the next imperative is spiritual progress.

Spiritual Progress

Scripture and Advancing Ethics

With the gospel we are equipped to bring ethical energy to bear on our families. It is no longer out of place to ask any question of ethical value or to invest in any love-motivated effort, for the good of family members. Beatitudinal values—meekness, tenderness ("those who mourn"), truth-hunger, mercy, sincerity ("pure in heart"), peacemaking, loyalty (Matt 5:3–12)—will build up families. These are society-building values. Already this was called for by the prophets: "He will turn the hearts of fathers to their children and the hearts of children to their fathers" (Mal 4:6 RSV; quoted in Luke 1:17). The love of God was explained on a basis of parental love: "Can a woman forget her nursing child, or show no compassion for the child of her womb? Even these may forget, yet I will not forget you" (Isa 49:15). "I will spare them as parents spare their children" (Mal 3:17). Jesus explains his own love on the basis of the Father's love: "As the Father has loved me, so I have loved you" (John 15:9).

These are biblical but not fundamentalist values. The recommended approach does not discard Scripture but combines Scripture with science. We are taking out of the storehouse things old and new (Matt 13:52), but nothing that we do not need, nothing that we have outgrown, nothing that is colored by abusive patterns. Admittedly, such abusiveness became so pervasive that we thought it was normal, but we know now that it is not normal to beat children. It is not healthy to be seething with resentment at one's children for their lack of appreciation; in fact, such resentment is itself a childish attitude. Too many parents are victims of their own childish resentments and are really unequipped for parenting. Spokespersons for cultural values should articulate the fact that parenting is not a program for gratifying the wounded narcissism of the would-be parents. It were better that a millstone were hung around your neck and you were thrown into the sea—or it were better that you seek intensive therapy. Do not use your children as puppets in your selfish psychodrama. Do not offend one of these little ones.

Some scriptural passages have been used to support authoritarian parenting concepts. God disciplines Israel "as a parent disciplines a child" (Deut 8:5). It is hardly adequate to account for the violence of God in many biblical passages by saying that God is *not always* abusive or that his brutality might diminish in the future.[48]

The violence in the Bible is a profound problem, but not an insurmountable one, if we have an evolutionary concept that can discern advances in ethics and theology from age to age, and that allows ancient people to have ideas appropriate to their level of cultural development. The kindliness of the prophets' God, who looks out for the defenseless and the abused,[49] is an advance on the idea that wealth and safety are evidence of God's favor.[50] The God of Second Isaiah, who created the Gentiles and enlightens them as well (Isa 42:5–6), is clearly more transcendent than the tribal Yahweh of the period of the Judges, and is truly *alone* as God. There is not really any Chemosh or Marduk for other nations, and certainly not a Moloch who calls for children to be passed through the fire.

Jesus offered the concept of the non-abusive parental God. The long gestation of Jesus' ideas within Western culture, along with natural cultural evolution, has issued in the present widespread interest in searching out non-abusive ways of parenting. The full significance of the dominical word about welcoming "one such child" and against despising "one of these little ones" (Matt 18:5, 10) is finally emerging.

Sanity and Progress

Our concept of God directly affects our ethics, including our whole approach toward child-rearing. Real sanity is related to making real spiritual progress. Parents learn this, if they have grown in the process of parenting, if they have practiced self-forgetful service. They certainly learn about the long-delayed expression of gratitude by children (usually *adult* children). Sometimes parenting remains largely a thankless job, and the joy of living seems to be crushed underfoot by the labor of living. But eventually the children grow, and parents get time to reflect. Hopefully, they can say "those who sow righteousness get a true reward" (Prov 11:18) or perhaps "those who sow in tears reap with shouts of joy" (Ps 126:5).

48. Stuart Lasine criticizes these views ("Divine Narcissism," 45).

49. Amos 2:6–7; Isa 58:6–7; Zech 7:10; and many more.

50. Ps 37:25, 37; Job 4:7; 36:11.

What would be the effect of a series of generations of healthy parenting within religious communities?—the emergence of a more spiritual civilization, where brotherly/sisterly love really does emanate from families, and spreads out to affect other institutions of society. The gospel helps families because it fosters "the integration of fathers into families . . . on the basis of a new ethic of equal regard."[51]

These can work against the pessimism toward which we might decline when we see how much cruelty and deformation of personality, how much suppression of thinking and stifling of love, how much manipulation and deceit, still takes place in many families. Is family really the best metaphor for our relationship to God? Are not families where the most painful abuse and injury occur? But it is precisely for that reason that the gospel focuses on the family—the site of the worst injury, the deepest gravity, the sharpest need, and the greatest hope. Like it or not, the family is the vestibule of future humanity.

The following chapter will delve into some of the cultural results of Jesus' gospel and values, after first looking at family structures in Jesus' times, and at his remarks about family.

51. Browning, *Marriage and Modernization*, 77–78.

FOUR

"Who are my mother and my brothers?"

Critique of Family

THIS CHAPTER BEGINS WITH a look at Jewish, Greek, and Roman family structures in the middle Hellenistic period (the time of Jesus). Then the radical remarks of Jesus and Paul about family can be considered within the context of their time and place. This is followed by some observations about the various approaches to family life taken by early Christians. There is a glance at Paul's radicalism (and Christianity's conservatism) on slavery. Finally, the centrality of family in Confucianism provides some basis for comparison.

Hellenistic Families

Families in Jesus' time were not the nuclear family of the modern West, with the mother and father being the only two adults in the home and the children moving out when they become adults. In the Hellenistic world, including Judea, most households centered around the father of an extended family, with his unmarried children and his married sons and their families living in the same household,[1] along with some of the father's unmarried brothers and sisters. The biblical phrase "the father's house" refers to this extended family, often situated in several houses around a common courtyard.[2] Married daughters would have moved out to live in the households

1. This is "patrilocal marriage" (Wenham, "Family in the Pentateuch," 18; also Carroll R., "Family in the Prophetic Literature," 105).

2. Wenham, "Family in the Pentateuch," 22; Carroll R., "Family in the Prophetic," 105–6.

of *their* husbands' fathers. Slaves, if there were any, were a part of the household, but did not figure in matters of lineage and inheritance. Nor was the home a thoroughly private place to which the members could go to escape from the workaday world. The home was a much more public place than that; it was "the place where much work was done, even among aristocrats," who also had to "entertain important people and conduct public business" there.[3]

There were substantial agreements, in this regard, between Jewish and Gentile households, although with interesting differences. Women were accorded considerable respect in Jewish households, although they were expected to be demure and to avoid public activity and politics. For centuries, the Jewish tradition had accorded a high respect to women, as evidenced by the large number of biblical stories of women playing important roles as prophets (Miriam, Huldah, Deborah, Isaiah's "prophetess" [Isa 8:3], and in the NT, Anna, some Corinthian women, and the daughters of Philip), warriors, queens, wives with considerable leadership within their households (Sarah, Rebecca), and women who took the initiative (Tamar, Rahab, Judith, Esther). The household could be called the "house of the mother" (Gen 24:28; Ruth 1:8; Song 3:4; 8:2; cf. Prov 14:1; 31:21–27), although "house of the father" was more common. The narrative books provide "numerous examples of the undermining of patriarchy."[4] We do not deny there was patriarchy in Hebrew society, but we deny that this was the whole story, or that the situation can be described simplistically. Mothers were to be respected.[5] The mother had considerable economic and social power. There was a thoroughgoing interdependence of males and females, with the latter having significant informal rights in the household, facts that are obscured if we focus only on the male-dominated stories of kingship and conquest.[6]

When we mention Israelite religion, we often think of temple and priests and the coronation and honoring of kings, but the religion of Israel underwent a long formative period within households and clans before there was a Hebrew monarchy.[7] The frequent reference to "the God of your [or 'my'] father" (Gen 26:24; 31:5; Exod 18:4) is evidence of this layer of

3. Osiek and Balch, *Families in the NT World,* 54.

4. Perdue, "Household, Old Testament Theology," 246.

5. Exod 20:12; 21:15; Lev 19:3; and many more. See Perdue, "The Israelite and Early Jewish Family," 182.

6. Meyers, *Discovering Eve,* 41–44; cf. 172–79.

7. See Albertz, *History of Israelite Religion,* 25–103. This is a masterful work.

religious experience. Albertz says this "typical family piety" is not so much an earlier stage as it is "a substratum of Yahweh religion."[8] This level of religion emphasizes intimacy with the deity; God is "like a father [who] protects the group"; there is no need of complex theology, much less tribalism, nationalism, or even "theological reflection."[9] Perdue looks at the ethically formative role of the family, arguing that the Hebrew ideals of "solidarity and community" emerged within the household: "The household was the theological lens, the ethical paradigm . . . for understanding . . . the activity of God and for living out moral responsibilities to others."[10]

Women had considerably lower status in most Greek households. The literary evidence from the Classical and early Hellenistic periods indicates that women were largely kept indoors, reckoned as attached to their fathers or husbands, and often treated with contempt. In the Classical period, Athenian girls were kept indoors, taught by their mothers and other women, trained to not ask questions about the outside world (Xenophon, *Oeconom.* 7.5), and married off at an early age by their "lord" (*kyrios*), their father or (if the father were dead) brother or grandfather.[11] Xenophon speaks of the women's rooms in Athenian homes being equipped with bolts and bars. A character in an Aristophanes play says "It is difficult for a (married) woman to escape from the home."[12] Many restrictions remained in place for city-dwelling Greeks in the Hellenistic period, with variations in law and custom from city to city but with a generally conservative trend being reinforced by restrictions on the right to citizenship, which strongly discouraged the city's natives from marrying outside their own population group.[13] Under the Roman empire, these strong local customs began to weaken, as people aspired to Roman citizenship. Intermarriage, and a concomitant loosening of strict customs, became widespread in the Roman empire.

In Roman society, women theoretically had this same secondary status, but in fact they often had considerably more power, as we will see. In Roman custom, an exceptional degree of authority was given to the male head of the super-family, the *paterfamilias*, even the power of life and death over his wife and children, although, by the imperial era, said power was no

8. Ibid., 29.

9. Ibid., 39.

10. Perdue, "Household, Old Testament Theology," 247–48.

11. Flacelière, *Daily Life in Greece*, 56–57.

12. Kitto, *The Greeks*, 219–20.

13. Thompson, "The Hellenistic Family," 98–100.

longer applicable to family but only to slaves.[14] The *paterfamilias* retained the power to arrange his children's marriages. There is peril in applying our term "family" to ancient households, since it could correspond to two very distinct terms in Latin. The *domus* is the household, which includes everybody living in the house, blood relatives or not, unmarried or not, slaves as well as free.[15] The more important idea, for the Romans, was *familia*, which refers to the descendants of a male bloodline.[16] Thus, slaves were part of the *domus*, of the household but not part of the *familia*,[17] having no biologic or legal significance; their parental pairings did not have the legal status of marriage.[18]

All of a Roman man's direct descendants were members of his *familia*, as were all the direct descendants of his sons but not his daughter's offspring, who would be members of the *familia* of her husband and her husband's father.[19] The authority of the *paterfamilias* was so great that it often caused serious problems. To some degree, a daughter married into her husband's (and her husband's father's) *familia*, but in fact, she was still technically under her father's control as long as he lived.[20] It was only her offspring who would be full members of that *familia* into which she had married. Both the woman's and her husband's power were limited as long as her father was alive, but the husband was the one most weakened by this arrangement. With time, women increasingly came to remain in their family of birth even after marriage, and this became the usual practice by the first century B.C.E.[21] Thus, many a Roman husband exercised *potestas* over everyone in the household except his wife.[22] Roman women, especially those of noble birth, thereby gained a relatively high degree of independence. Further, a widow's right to get her dowry back contributed to the power of

---

14. Osiek and Balch, *Families in the NT World*, 57.

15. Saller, *Patriarchy, Property and Death*, 82.

16. Garnsey and Saller, *The Roman Empire*, 127–28; Dixon, *The Roman Family*, 3–4.

17. In usage, however, these terms were less than precise; *domus* could also refer to the larger extended family, including distant relatives (Saller, *Patriarchy, Property and Death*, 84–88).

18. Dixon, *The Roman Family*, 58.

19. Ibid., 73; Garnsey and Saller, *The Roman Empire*, 127.

20. Dixon, *The Roman Family*, 41; Garnsey and Saller, *The Roman Empire*, 130; Saller, *Patriarchy, Property and Death*, 76.

21. Dixon, *The Roman Family*, 44.

22. Osiek and Balch, *Families in the NT World*, 61.

Roman women.[23] Thus, the irony of this highly patriarchal system was that it ended up conferring significant power on women of the noble classes.

The mixing of cultures caused stress around the subject of customs and morals, especially for a strongly religious culture such as the Jewish culture. The partially-Jewish Herodian rulers attempted to straddle the Jewish and Roman worlds; when the Herodian wives flouted Jewish tradition and displayed the freedom typical of Roman noblewomen, they evoked criticism from such people as John the Baptizer[24] and the Jewish historian Josephus.[25]

Jesus' Radical Remarks

Why do we care about all these details of family structure? Knowledge of how conservative these cultures were draws into sharp relief how radical—and risky—Jesus' sayings were. It would be hard to find anything in all of Jewish literature as radical as Jesus' remark to a man whose father had recently died, and who wanted to stay and perform the necessary funerary rituals before leaving to follow Jesus—"let the dead bury their own dead" (Matt 8:22; Luke 9:60). Following Jesus may mean abandoning those duties that custom holds most sacred! Like Jesus' other most radical remarks about family and religious loyalties, this one concerns the unique obligations of an apostle. The "let the dead" saying immediately follows one that refers to itinerant living: "the Son of Man has nowhere to lay his head" (Matt 8:20; Luke 9:58). It is evidently the full-time apostle, not the average disciple, who has no time for such time-consuming activity as burial rituals and the traditional period of mourning.

It is the traveling apostle who has "left everything and followed you" (Matt 19:27). Jesus promises only an eschatological reward for apostles: "everyone who has left houses or brothers or sisters or father or mother or children or fields, for my name's sake, will receive a hundredfold, and will inherit eternal life" (Matt 19:29). This quotation reveals an important difference between the Synoptic Gospels. Matthew and Mark (10:29) do not mention any leaving of wife or husband, but Luke does: "who has left house or wife" (18:29). We will encounter some surprisingly harsh wording

23. Dixon, *The Roman Family*, 74.

24. Matt 12:3–4; Mark 6:17–19.

25. Josephus *Ant.* 15.259; 17.341; 18.136. See Hanson and Oakman, *Palestine in the Time of Jesus*, 42.

in Luke, because he has an agenda on this topic; he "promotes ascetic values."[26] This leads him to put more extreme words into Jesus' mouth. Only Luke's Jesus says that one must "hate [*misei*] father and mother, wife and children, brothers and sisters, yes, and even life itself" in order to "be my disciple" (Luke 14:26). Matthew probably gives us something closer to Jesus' actual words, stressing the *greater* importance of loyalty to the divine, without condemning loyalty to family: "Whoever loves father or mother more than me is not worthy of me" (Matt 10:37). The point is the right *priority* between spiritual and earthly loyalties,[27] not an *extreme severence* of spiritual loyalties from all earthly ones. Matthew and Mark seem closer than Luke to Jesus' thinking when they reflect the *desirability* of brothers and sisters and parents, who are promised to be restored "a hundredfold" (Matt 19:29; Mark 10:30).

As in all historical Jesus research, we have to take note of how the message of Jesus was shaped, adapted, and distorted by the evangelists, and also (and earlier) by his immediate circle of followers. The distortion (or personal creativity) will be greatest with issues that are emotionally charged for the evangelist concerned: for Mark, it is the extraordinary notion of a suffering Messiah; for Matthew, there are two charged issues here—the significance of Jewish law and of Jewish rejection of Jesus, and the concept of the church as a brotherhood;[28] for Luke, the sharp issues are wealth, injustice, and asceticism versus family. Taking note of such factors, we can tease out the basics of the historical Jesus' teaching.

Again, the "love father or mother" saying concerns full-time evangelists. It is they who must turn away from family obligations in order to travel and preach. In the material leading up to this saying, we see Jesus speaking to "these twelve," who will be traveling and preaching in "town or village" where he is "sending you out" (Matt 10:5, 11, 16). "Sending out" is *apostellō*, from which the cognate noun, *apostle*, is derived. The saying concerns the special duties and personal sacrifices of apostles. Jesus warns that some family members may turn against the apostles (10:21, 35–37), and this is where they are warned that their primary loyalties are to Jesus and to God (10:37, 40). He is giving fair warning to anyone who would become an apostle. In addition, the apostles may have intensified Jesus' words in

---

26. Osiek and Balch, *Families in the NT World*, 136.

27. Barton, *Discipleship and Family Ties*, 122, 221–22.

28. On church brotherhood in Matthew see ibid., 148–49, 217–19.

the heat of battle, that is, in the experience of having to *make* these difficult personal sacrifices, and in their retelling of the story of their calling.

Some sayings echo the style of the shocking but realistic warnings of the Hebrew prophets. Such a warning is the mournful prophecy of the coming destruction of Jerusalem: "Woe to those who are pregnant and to those who are nursing infants in those days! Pray that it may not be in winter" (Mark 13:17–18). Jesus' sorrow is real, responding to particular sorrows to come. There are real dangers of the Gospel turning "a man against his father . . . daughter against her mother" (Matt 10:35). Discord will be the consequence of families taking offense at the fact that a family member places his or her fundamental loyalty in God's work, rather than in the earth family. Again Jesus shows that he is quite aware of the painful particulars of human experience.

One aspect of Jesus' saying would have sounded familiar to some. The idea of "the subordination of family ties for the sake of a higher good" was already widespread in both Judaism and Gentile philosophy.[29] Such a point was frequently made by sages—Jewish, Cynic, and Stoic—though with less of a tone of compassionate warning than we see in Jesus.

But there are also some remarks of Jesus that seem cruel, and that seem to marginalize family ties, as in his rude response to his mother and siblings on one occasion: "Who are my mother and my brothers?" (Mark 3:33). We need to notice the setting. Jesus' family members arrived at a house where Jesus was preaching and "they sent to him and called him" (Mark 3:31). Discussions of this passage often overlook the fact that they were interrupting his preaching, seeking a public salute of honor from him. They presumed that blood-relation gave them status and that Jesus would stop his preaching and acknowledge them. Jesus always responds to interruptions on the basis of their motivation; when one's motives are sincere, there is no danger in interrupting him. One can grab his cloak if one needs healing. One can even tear open the roof above his head and let down a man on a pallet. These are gospel-motives. But the quest for adulation is a selfish motive, and it spurred Jesus' indignation:

> "Who are my mother and my brothers?" And looking at those who
> sat around him, he said, "Here are my mother and my brothers!

29. Balch, "Paul, Families, and Households," 266–67; Barton, *Discipleship and Family Ties*, 221; Hellerman, *Ancient Church as Family*, 61–62 (on God-loyalty over family-loyalty in Deut 13:6–9).

Whoever does the will of God is my brother and sister and mother" (Mark 3:33–35).

A more important bond than that of biology is the permanent bond among those who have made the eternal commitment to God's way. The selfish desire of his mother and brothers to receive acknowledgement from Jesus while he was in the middle of doing important work dramatizes the inferiority of earthly ties when people allow their desire for honor to interfere with spiritual work. Jesus is showing a higher loyalty, one that sets out to conquer the disease of selfishness in individuals *and* in families.

There is no denying the witness of the Synoptic Gospels that Jesus was in high tension with his own kin, that he trained his apostles to "give his mission a higher priority than the love of their family," and that they went on to form "alternate 'kinship' relations with fellow believers outside the family circle."[30] Subsequent Christianity was "remarkably ambiguous" about the traditional structures of family life[31]—but only when they threatened to stand in the way of the work of spreading the larger "family" message—the gospel.

Jesus is really breaking "with the traditional role of children within the family" when he uses "children as 'role models.'"[32] Jesus has an interest in real families and real children, but his primary focus is on ultimate loyalty to the kingdom of God, which is the responsibility of the individual: "go into your room and shut the door and pray to your Father who is in secret" (Matt 6:6). Sincere individual devotion will empower one to judge truthfully: "Anyone who resolves to do the will of God will know whether the teaching is from God" (John 7:17).

Let us notice this important clause "do the will of God," which is virtually a summary of Jesus' teaching. It is to be noted that he considers people to *have the capacity* to not only make this choice, but to fulfill it. Entrance to the kingdom of heaven depends upon doing the will of God (Matt 7:21). Do we realize the faith that Jesus has *in us*, that he does not doubt that we are capable of doing the will of God? There is nothing here about humans being totally depraved or being unable to do the will of God (*contra* Augustine, Luther, Calvin). The God-receptive person *can* discern God's will and way (John 1:46; 7:17; 8:47; Luke 8:15; Rom 12:2), and it will set him free (John 8:32–36). A good person has a good heart, and the pure in heart will

---

30. Barclay, "Family as the Bearer of Religion," 74.

31. Ibid., 72.

32. Moxnes, "What is Family?," 34.

see God (Luke 6:45; Matt 5:8); if yours is not clean, then "First clean the inside of the cup," or "make the tree good" (Matt 23:26; 12:33). One ought to practice "justice and the love of God" (Luke 11:42), to love God and neighbor (Mark 12:30–31). Jesus quotes the boldest OT passages that speak of people being taught by God (John 6:45 [Isa 54:13]); *being* gods, which probably means having divine qualities (John 10:34 [Ps 82:6]);[33] praying together with people of all nations (Mark 11:17 [Isa 56:7]); having living waters in the heart (John 7:38 [Isa 12:3; 58:11]).

Having such spiritual capacities, people ought not to dwell just on the level of materiality and biology. We see him again pointing out the priority of the spiritual over the biologic when a woman shouts out "Blessed is the womb that bore you and the breasts that nursed you!" Jesus corrects her by saying "Blessed rather are those who hear the word of God and obey it!" (Luke 11:27–28). Nothing can surpass the relationship to God, not even the pride and joy of motherhood. Biologic ties will not confer any special status in the kingdom of God.

We should also notice that many sayings and actions of Jesus assume the goodness of family affection. Even his remarks about having to leave one's family have a pro-family assumption: he promises them "a hundred-fold now in this age—houses, brothers and sisters, mothers and children" (Mark 10:30).[34] If family were something bad, this would be a threat rather than a promise.[35] Instead, Jesus is the "householder" over a new "'spiritual' family."[36] Clearly, having brothers and sisters and mothers is understood to be a good thing.

Jesus was showing the true relation between divine reality and human reality: the human family is not absolute but is meant to follow a divine pattern. One could even say that family language is not really metaphorical, but that the earthly family itself is a metaphor, that is, a reflection, of divine *reality*. The family becomes the best metaphor for picturing the divine reality of care-taking, love, and growth. The family metaphor pictures something that precedes and exceeds the family. The author of Ephesians knew this: "I bow my knees before the Father, from whom every family in heaven and on earth takes its name" (Eph 3:14–15).

33. On John 10:34, see Finlan, "Deification in Jesus' Teaching," 31–33.

34. Mark sees it happening "now in this age," while Matt 19:29 and Luke 18:30 defer it to "eternal life."

35. See Barton, *Discipleship and Family Ties*, 122, 217.

36. Barton, *Discipleship and Family Ties*, 218.

Of course, Jesus gives much evidence of his positive feelings about family: he attends weddings, uses wedding parties in his parables, calls himself a bridegroom, and even appoints John bar Zebedee as his replacement in his biologic family.[37] Jesus assumes and defends the household, as seen in his prohibition of divorce and his indignant remarks about using religion as an excuse to withhold support from one's aging parents (Mark 10:4–12; 7:9–13).[38]

One can hardly doubt that Jesus loved his family. But he made it clear that one's loyalty to God was more important even than family loyalties. The often selfish claims of family members must not be allowed to interfere with one's religious mission. The irony of using family metaphors for the gospel is that they only work if one's loyalty to God is primary, yet one retains a strong, but secondary, loyalty to one's earth family.

This differs from the Cynic position, which really rejects social institutions like marriage. The Cynic position was spiritually honest and serious, holding that genuine religious loyalty *has* to criticize family, if it is to articulate true loyal to the transcendent God. Unfortunately, as human philosophies usually do, Cynicism became rigid and dualistic, maintaining a radical opposition between philosophy and family. The forsaking of married life for the higher life of the sage was also an important theme for some Stoics. It is best to remain unmarried, "wholly devoted to the service of God."[39] Philo of Alexandria had these same dualistic tendencies, approving of those Levites who "acknowledge no love nor kinship but God's love."[40]

Christianity need not follow such a dualistic pattern. Even the most pro-family religion needs to critique family, since family ideologies tend to make totalizing claims and to serve the needs of whoever has the most power in the family. We *need* the religious "force that *both affirms and judges* the inherent limits of familial loyalty"; the family does not automatically and effortlessly move "towards a universal fraternity."[41]

Of course, Jesus is setting out to establish a spiritual family, one that will include the earth families, but only if the religious idea is strong enough to maintain itself and exert its influence on culture. The kingdom of

37. John 2:1–10; Matt 22:1–14; 25:1–13; 9:15; Luke 5:34; 12:36; 14:8; John 19:26–27.

38. See Barton, "Relativization of Family Ties," 96.

39. Epictetus, *Diss.* 3.22.69–72, 81; cited in Barton, "Revitalization of Family Ties," 95.

40. *Spec. Leg.* 3.124–26; cited in Barton, "Relativization of Family Ties," 87.

41. Waters, *Family in Christian Social*, 52.

God is fundamentally the *family* of God, a network of permanent spiritual affiliations.

Paul's Radicalism

We come to the church's most influential theologian, Paul the apostle, and to a consideration both of his metaphorical family language and of his attitude toward family life. I wish to begin by supporting the remarks of Joseph Hellerman, who notes that Paul's ethics extend the brother-sister loyalty values of the ancient patrilineal kinship family. Hellerman argues that scholars like E. Castelli and S. Moore have it exactly wrong when they say that Paul's kinship terminology indicates his attempt to impose strict hierarchic control: "Rather, those who had the most to gain from the image of the church as family were the poor, the hungry, the enslaved, the imprisoned"; the terminology of brother and sister "had nothing to do with hierarchy . . . but everything to do with equality, solidarity" and loyalty to the "faith family."[42] The call for brotherly behavior means sharing, forgiving, and extending honor and respect to all. Hellerman argues that modern scholars are engaging in autobiography rather than in exegesis when they detect cruelty, disrespect, and alienation in Paul's kinship language. Even much of the imagery of the cross has an ethical focus. "Paul employs the symbol of the rejection and humiliation of Jesus in order to attack the oppression of low status church members."[43] "Paul viewed the Jesus community in Philippi as a family,"[44] and his whole purpose is to encourage sympathy and love to function, as in a healthy family.

Others have discerned that Paul's "brother" language places people "on the same plane," even Onesimus and Philemon.[45] This is not to deny that Paul exerts his authority, not least in Philemon, where he pressures the slave owner to take back Onesimus, "no longer as a slave but more than a slave, a beloved brother" (Phlm 1:16). Paul uses his authority to assert *familial* values.

We must assess Paul's position on sexuality and marriage, which relies on a worldview in which Spirit and flesh war against each other. Writing to the Corinthians, Paul allows married life as an acceptable alternative to

42. Hellerman, *Ancient Church as Family*, 221; cf. 217–18.

43. Ibid., 219.

44. Hellerman, "Brothers and Friends," 23.

45. Porter, "Family in the Epistles," 157.

"immorality" (1 Cor 7:2), but it is clear that marriage is second best. The married person is "bound," and marriage leads to "distress" and "anxieties" (7:27–28, 32). It is those who "are not practicing self-control" who "should marry" (1 Cor 7:9). Celibacy would be better: "I wish that all were as I myself am" (1 Cor 7:7).

There is a fundamental conflict, for Paul, between flesh and Spirit: "For what the flesh desires is opposed to the Spirit" (Gal 5:17). There is no neutrality on this issue; true loyalty to God and Christ means a thorough repudiation of the flesh: "those who belong to Christ Jesus have crucified the flesh with its passions and desires" (Gal 5:24). Paul did not go to the impossible extremes that later churchmen did, telling married couples to avoid feeling any pleasure during the sex act. Paul is not so wedded to a strange abstraction. He was realistic about, and even considerate of, the needs of married people, advising against long periods of sexual abstinence within marriage (1 Cor 7:5). Further, a believer can move an unbelieving partner to conversion (1 Cor 7:14–16). Even so, the apostle's negative view of sexuality is apparent: "do not gratify the desires of the flesh" (Gal 5:16).

He is probably not trying to get men and women to extinguish desire but to turn away from a fundamentally selfish motivation (the way of the flesh) to a fundamentally Godly one (the way of the Spirit). One will either "set the mind on the flesh, [which] is death" or "on the Spirit, [which] is life and peace" (Rom 8:6). The mind that is set on the flesh cannot obey God, cannot please God (Rom 8:7–8). Thus, Paul's message is psychologically and spiritually deep, is realistic yet idealistic. But there is no doubt that its expression is drastically dualistic: "if by the Spirit you put to death the deeds of the body, you will live" (Rom 8:13). So it is not so surprising, after all, that the later church (made up of people much less original and much more literal-minded than Paul) would come up with an extreme asceticism that condemns even normal marital pleasure.

Religious idealism often creates intense moral dualisms that are stressful and psychologically damaging to later generations. A severe spiritual distress can dwell at the heart of religious intensity, usually because of a philosophic failure, a lapse in comprehension of reality, which then leads to an impossibly demanding idealism. The philosophic failure at the heart of the idealism that sets sexuality against spirituality is an unconscious materialism: it pulls God down to the material level and says: "you must *either* be spiritual or sexual; you must *either* follow God or follow normal life; you cannot do both." But this is a tragic misunderstanding of spirituality (which is not *one* area of our life, but is an attitude we carry through all areas of our life) and of God (who is not in competition with the material level and who seeks to permeate even our material lives). Here I am restating the argument of Alan Watts, who said that to make God and nature incompatible is to bring God down to the level of his creatures. It is to treat the knowledge of God and the knowledge of creatures as though they were the same kind of knowledge, and therefore in competition with each other. But knowledge of God is universal; it can include all other kinds of knowledge, and should not be set against them.[46]

Paul is well aware of the presence of God in every moment of his life, but it seems that he does begin to make this mistake of setting God against certain normal functions of life. He has a deep suspicion about the world, the "age," and the desire-nature within people. "The works of the flesh are . . . fornication, impurity . . . strife . . . envy" (Gal 5:19–21). We need the Messiah to die "for our sins to set us free from the present evil age" (Gal 1:4). His spiritual optimism is bonded to an intense pessimism about human nature: "The god of this world has blinded the minds of the unbelievers" (2 Cor 4:4). People are "the ungodly" (Rom 4:5; 5:6).

Paul has many other things to say. He speaks of transformation of mind, enabling one to discern the will of God and to "have the mind of Christ" (Rom 12:2; Phil 1:9–10; 2:5; 1 Cor 2:16). He teaches transformation into the image of Christ (2 Cor 3:18; 4:6; Rom 8:29), who himself "is the image of God" (2 Cor 4:4). In fact, Paul was too complicated and many-sided for his successors to understand. But they were fully capable of taking quite literally his teaching about "our sinful passions" (Rom 7:5).

In the institution-building period of Christianity, a hierarchy of ascetics over the married emerges. The next several centuries witness a sharpening of the attitude that exalts celibacy as spiritually superior to sexual activity. A compromise is worked out wherein "the weak-willed majority" are allowed to marry, while accepting the leadership of "the more spiritualized elite," the celibates.[47] This goes beyond what Paul taught, but then the church exaggerated and altered most of what Paul taught, especially his concept of Christ's death as an atoning action.

Paul did plant some seeds that lesser minds cultivated into plants that lacked balanced beauty but highlighted one or another aspect of the apostle's teaching, especially his asceticism, which was a widespread religious

46. Watts, *Nature, Man and Woman*, 150.
47. Newman, *Biblical Religion and Family Values*, 162.

trend at the time. It seems that the Mediterranean world was experiencing a metaphysical crisis about the relationship between spirituality and physicality, and was taking an increasingly negative view toward the latter. The gospel did not require such a negative attitude. It *did* require a reassessment of the place of marriage and family, but Christians came up with different and competing solutions.

Three Responses to Family

It may be that three distinct responses to family emerge from taking the gospel seriously:

- *Rejectionist:* Strongly asserts spiritual loyalties *instead* of family loyalties, since the latter are often in competition with the higher loyalties expected of a kingdom believer.

- *Subordinationist:* Subordinates the literal family to a metaphorical one: exalting the church *as family*; this entails a valuation of family-like relationships but not necessarily in connection with literal families; often it has been close-knit sects or religious orders that have most thoroughly embodied the church-as-family metaphor.

- *Affirmative:* Affirms marriage and family, connecting them with an image of the family of God, the latter signifying either the worldwide church or the whole universe of humans and angels who worship God. This option thinks of the household as the basic unit of Christian community and of the church as a community *of families*. At first glance, this option may look like the healthiest, but we need to notice that it tends to compromise with the surrounding culture, assimilating to the dominant household structures. This option involved making significant compromise with the strongly patriarchal Hellenistic family structure of the time.

The first option affirms holy asceticism, the second affirms membership in a brotherhood, the third uplifts both literal and metaphorical family. When Rowan Greer writes that the NT shows "attitudes that now reject, now supplant, and now affirm the family,"[48] he seems to be referring to the same three options. If we follow Greer, we would say that the Gospel of Matthew has the strongest rejectionist strain; "the impact of the Gospel

48. Greer, *Broken Lights and Mended Lives*, 97.

shatters the family"; the believer "can call no one his father on earth" and may become a eunuch for the kingdom.[49] Matthew 19:12 does, indeed, express support for asceticism (becoming "eunuchs for the sake of the kingdom"). Nevertheless, I think that Matthew fits equally well in the second category, because of its strong stress on brotherhood. Different passages can be used to put Matthew in either category. Greer enlists 23:9 ("call no one your father on earth") in putting Matthew in the rejectionist camp, but I find as much here to put it in the "supplanting" group, for the verse continues "you have one Father—the one in heaven," and it was preceded by "you are all brothers" (Matt 23:8 NAB, mistranslated "students" by the NRSV). The family metaphor is the controlling image there, which is characteristic of the second category.

I find a similar dual categorization for Paul, who is himself an ascetic (1 Cor 7:1, 7–8, 38), but who is the great spokesman for the second option, the development of devoted fellowships of "brothers and sisters" who "bear one another's burdens" (Gal 5:13; 6:2) and who "outdo one another in showing honor" (Rom 12:10). Ephesians, the Pastoral Epistles, and First Peter embody the family-affirming option,[50] but they also occasionally utilize the metaphorical language of brotherhood.[51]

The brotherhood metaphor of the second option is seen to permeate the other two options, and since neither Matthew nor Paul fit comfortably within one model, it may be more helpful to recognize the second "model" as the social essence of Christianity itself: transforming human relationships with the spirit and the imagery of brotherhood, under the tutelage of the heavenly Father. If we recognize this as the core of the social teaching of Christianity, present in *all* its main branches, we are left with only two competing models, one that places a high value on asceticism and sets holiness in some tension with traditional families (Matthew, Luke, Paul, and Revelation), and one that reaffirms the prevailing family roles and turns away from asceticism (the deutero-Pauline and Petrine letters). Mark leans mildly toward the ascetic end; the Gospel of John leans toward the affirmative option.

The historical Paul is at the opposite pole from the deutero-Paulines (the successors to Paul) on this point. Compare Paul's notion of "sinful passions . . . at work in our members to bear fruit for death" (Rom 7:5) with

---

49. Ibid.; Matt 10:34–39; 23:9; 8:22; 19:12.

50. Eph 5:22–27; 1 Tim 2:15; 5:4, 14; 1 Pet 3:1–6.

51. 1 Pet 5:9, 12; Eph 6:21.

the dogma in First Timothy 2:15: woman "will be saved through childbearing [*teknogonia*]." Among the competitors for Paul's legacy, the group that emerged victorious was vigorously conservative, and we see it especially in the Pastoral Epistles—First and Second Timothy, and Titus—probably the most successful and influential forged letters in human history. They undo Paul's asceticism (1 Tim 4:3; 5:23) and curtail the activities of women in the church (1 Tim 2:11–15; 4:7; 5:13–14; 2 Tim 3:6–7; Titus 2:3–5).[52] An institutional church could not accept a complex and radical Paul. It needed a "Saint Paul," an authority figure who could be made to approve the authority structure (male overseers, elders, and deacons) that was emerging in the church. The deutero-Pauline letters domesticate Paul, making him a eunuch for their kingdom. We will examine more of these alterations shortly.

Changed Households

It is difficult to document all the effects that the teaching of Jesus had on family life in the early generations of Christianity. As we see from our three options, his teaching really had more than one effect, *each* of which involved a heightened sense of the family-like nature of the relationship with God. This is the central fact. All versions of orthodox Christianity[53] used family-language to describe the relationship with God and with other believers. The extent of this *religious focus on familiarity* was unprecedented. Those who served were brothers. Women, including those who hosted churches, were sisters. Older Christians were affectionately called mother or father. God was father; Jesus was both a father and an elder brother, and yet had motherly qualities. Later, Mother Mary would become an important figure.

Women and children enjoyed enhanced status in many early Christian households, although our evidence is sketchy. Christians, like Jews, rejected the practice of exposing unwanted infants, which resulted in the survival of more female children.[54] In assessing the changes in the status of women and children, we should avoid constructing a picture of an egalitarian Christian

---

52. Regarding the competition for Paul's legacy, see Young, *Theology of the Pastoral Epistles*, 14–23; and Finlan, *Apostle Paul and the Pauline Tradition*, 166–78.

53. In distinction from proto-Gnostic groups. The *Gospel of Thomas*, for instance, prefers to speak of the believer as "the solitary one" or the one who has "light" (Sayings 11, 16, 24, 49, 50, 61, 75, 77). "Brother" terminology occurs only in passages that are probably derived from the canonical Gospels (Sayings 25, 26, 55, 99).

54. Westfall, "Family in the Gospels and Acts," 128–29.

household in contrast to a stereotype of a patriarchal Jewish household. In fact, much of the high ethics of Christianity comes from Jewish family life. For instance, the Jewish "*ketubah* (marriage contract . . . did protect women's rights)."[55]

The more glaring contrast is between Christian households and *Gentile* ones. The philosopher Celsus attacks Christianity for allowing a high degree of independence for women and children, and their involvement in what we would call evangelism. He says Christians tell children "that they must not pay any attention to their fathers and schoolteachers . . . they say [they] know the right way to live, and if the children would believe them, they would become happy and make their home happy as well. . . . [I]f they like, they should leave father and schoolmasters, and go along with the women" to the shops to spread their "empty chatter."[56] Evangelism is here attacked as a plan for undermining male authority figures and raising the independence of women and young people. Despite the distortion, this attack constitutes evidence for the heightened status of women and young people within the home and for their involvement in the spread of Christianity.

It seems that Gentile women were strongly attracted to the Christians' valuation of marriage and children and their rejection of infanticide, abortion, and easy divorce.[57] Browning's assessment is insightful: "Christianity never completely escaped the patriarchy of antiquity, [but] it clearly fractured it"; in place of the Aristotelian notion that wives should be subordinate, it taught "mutual subordination between husband and wife."[58] Christianity demanded a fundamental change in men's attitudes, presenting the new and demanding "image of male servanthood," which was a revolutionary change for both men and women. [59]

Of course, such changes in family ethics did not happen uniformly throughout early Christian communities. Further, the changes are interpreted in differing ways. Unlike Celsus, Luke, the author of Acts, pictures the Christian message functioning within existing family structures. "The

---

55. Levine, "Theological Education," 333.

56. From Origen's *Contra Celsum* 3.55, quoted in MacDonald, "Was Celsus Right?," 157–58.

57. Stark, *Rise of Christianity*, 111, 117, 210; Browning, *Marriage and Modernization*, 62–63, 65.

58. Browning, *Marriage and Modernization*, 69–70.

59. Ibid., 70–71.

conversion of households"[60] is a programmatic theme for Luke. He pictures Christianity as stabilizing the household, perhaps to soothe any fears that the family was being undermined.[61] Yet Luke also names more women than any other gospel, some of whom were financial patrons of the Jesus movement (Luke 8:2–3), and in Acts many "leading women" and "Greek women and men of high standing" follow Paul (Acts 17:4, 12).

In sum, literary sources give evidence for significant changes in family structures in the first two centuries of Christianity: Jesus' startling focus on children; women being the first witnesses of the resurrection in all the Gospels; and the prominence of women in the very different testimonies of Luke, Celsus, Paul, and the successors to Paul.

Resistance to Change

Ironically, another strong piece of evidence for the changes in Christian households is the strong resistance to change by some who want to preserve the traditional Greek and Roman household. Dampening the radical tendencies of Jesus and Paul, the Pastoral Epistles put the Christian stamp of approval upon the authoritative status of the *paterfamilias*, the segregation of groups by age and sex, the silencing of "older women" (Titus 2:3), and suspicion about "silly women" (2 Tim 3:6), "old wives' tales" (1 Tim 4:7), and certain "teachers" (1 Tim 1:7; 2 Tim 4:3). Some of the teachers probably *are* women—"younger widows" who go about from house to house as "gossips and busybodies" and who should, instead, "marry, bear children, and manage their households" (1 Tim 5:11–14). Women should be "submissive to their husbands" (Titus 2:5). These letters are busily "'re-patriarchising' early Christian communities."[62]

The "Paul" of these letters says "I permit no woman to teach or to have authority over a man" (1 Tim 2:12). The author takes the name of Paul and claims control of the Pauline heritage, ignoring the fact that Paul mentions many women leaders, and even one female apostle, by name (Rom 16:1–7, 13–15 ["Junia" is in v. 7]; 1 Cor 16:19; Phil 4:2–3).

The pastor also wants a hierarchy of age: the young need to be under the authority of those older men and women who are "sober, serious, and

60. MacDonald, "Was Celsus Right?," 177.

61. "Christians were upsetting the civic culture by giving their wives more freedom" (Browning, *Equality and the Family*, 45).

62. Moxnes, "What is Family?," 33.

moderate" and who show the younger men and women how to behave. The pastor thinks of the church as "the household of God" (1 Tim 3:15),[63] and of the Christian household as "a church in microcosm."[64] He takes the ethical obligations within the biologic family so seriously that anyone who does not provide for his family (*oikeioi*) is worse than an unbeliever (1 Tim 5:8).

Of course, all of this may be seen as a normal and expected social strategy for a minority religion threatened by potential repression from the prevailing culture. One can notice in the pastor's community all the features that are typical of a sectarian in-group, an emphasis on "harmony, obedience to authority . . . always doing what is proper" and on "virtues such as a sense of shame, filial piety, respect for the social order, self-discipline, concern for social recognition . . . public image."[65] In observing how the church toned down Jesus' teachings, assimilating them to prevailing (Gentile) social norms, there is some danger of the twenty-first century individualist feeling contempt for this community. It would be better to extend some consideration to these people who felt in danger. Still, it needs to be stated that the pastor's community did, in fact, domesticate and undermine many of Jesus' teachings.

The Pastorals strongly affirm salvation through Christ. This is where they are uncompromising. Perhaps the other compromises were necessary for survival as a minority religion in an age that was suspicious of new religions. Craig Keener says that minority religions often had "to demonstrate their lack of subversiveness"; this would explain the obsessive emphasis on proper order in the Pastorals, showing that Christians were not out "to radically overturn Roman social structures."[66] This strategy seems to have worked, enabling this branch of orthodox Christianity to continue expanding, and to eventually be appealing enough to be chosen by Roman emperors.

One way to appreciate the enormity of the difference between the Pastorals and Paul is to examine what lies halfway between them, the first stage in the domestication and redefinition of Paul, the deutero-Pauline letter to the Ephesians. The ancestor text to Ephesians is Colossians, which has a good possibility of having been co-authored by Paul. Ephesians moves the

63. Barclay, "There is Neither Old Nor Young?," 237.

64. Barclay, "Family as the Bearer of Religion," 77.

65. Malina, *Social Gospel of Jesus*, 125. He is describing strongly collectivist groups, not the pastor's community in particular.

66. Keener, *Paul, Women & Wives*, 146–47.

discourse of Colossians in a more conformist direction. The advice to not cause children to "lose heart" (Col 3:21) is dropped from the parallel passage in Ephesians (6:4). Ephesians is still fairly close to Paul theologically and in time of composition, but is definitely more socially conservative than the undisputed letters of Paul (1 Thess; Gal; 1–2 Cor; Rom; Phlm; Phil).

Nevertheless, mutuality and consideration are major themes in Ephesians. The advice to fathers is quite remarkable for its time: "fathers, do not provoke your children to anger" (Eph 6:4). The advice to married couples is even more unusual for the ancient world: "be subject to one another" (5:21). Husbands are to "love your wives, just as Christ loved the church and gave himself up for her" (5:25)—but the marriage relationship is still hierarchical: "The husband is the head of the wife just as Christ is the head of the church . . . as the church is subject to Christ, so also wives ought to be, in everything, to their husbands" (5:23–24). Similarly, even though masters should "stop threatening" their slaves (6:9)—the hierarchic relation remains: "slaves, obey your earthly masters with fear and trembling" (6:5).[67] Browning says the Ephesians' passage, asking husbands to love their wives as Christ loves the church, "reverses the image of the dominant and aggressive male."[68]

Although Ephesians retains something of Jesus' and Paul's strikingly new teaching on kindliness, it is placed within a family that retains some patriarchal power structure. The father, exhorted to love and not to provoke, is still the hierarch in the family. Husbands' consideration for their wives (Eph 5:25; Col 3:19) is undergirded with wifely subjection (Eph 5:23–24; Col 3:18).

Parental non-provoking (Eph 6:4; Col 3:21) does not replace the advice to children, "obey your parents" (Eph 6:1; Col 3:20). This is a "benevolent patriarchy . . . male authority . . . has overshadowed the demand to receive children as gifts."[69] The degree of compromise with Gentile patriarchal forms is, in my view, significantly worse in the Pastoral Epistles. There is nothing in the Pastorals about husbands and wives being subject to one another, about fathers not provoking children, about masters not threatening slaves (Col 3:21; Eph 6:4; 6:9) or needing to treat them justly (Col 4:1).

---

67. It is unclear whether slaves were to submit to masters' sexual advances. This issue was probably "not yet sorted out as something to reject explicitly" (Osiek, "Female Slaves," 274). Clearly, Christian masters are to treat slaves justly (Col 4:1).

68. Browning, *Equality and the Family*, 44.

69. Miller-McLemore, *Let the Children Come*, 87–88.

Unfortunately, the authoritarian Pastorals probably had more influence than Ephesians, at least in the first eighteen centuries. The appearance of Bushnell's *Christian Nurture* marked a reassertion of the ethic of mutuality, with accompanying sensitivity to children. (See the section "Spirituality, Respect" in chapter 3.)

Browning does not deny the facts of the Pastorals' reversal of many of Jesus' and Paul's reforms, but he tends to emphasize the positive effects even of compromised Christianity. He certainly is correct that "the Jesus movement subtly resisted" patriarchal forms,[70] and that Christianity sought to impress fatherly duty upon men. One of the strengths of Christianity is that it "functions to counteract deep male ambivalence about joining the mother-infant family."[71]

Competition in the Pauline Tradition

The Pastoral Epistles' authoritarian family was not the only model that existed within the Pauline tradition. A very different alternative uplifted celibacy as an expression of religious devotion and purity, especially for women. The apocryphal Acts, despite their many fantastic ingredients, do testify to a phenomenon of enthusiastic women celibates whose choices were upsetting to the men in their lives: their betrothed, their husbands, their fathers. It appears that one of the three main branches of the deutero-Pauline tradition was an ascetic movement that included women leaders. This branch lost out to the branch that gave us the Pastoral Epistles, where women who "forbid marriage" are attacked (1 Tim 4:3). A third branch, the gnostic (or proto-gnostic) one, may also have had some women leaders, even though it shared a common viewpoint that equated rationality and philosophy with the male and squalid earthliness with the female. The last line of the *Gospel of Thomas* says that Mary has to become male to enter the kingdom of heaven (Saying 114).

Observing the branch represented by the Pastorals, Margaret Mac-Donald is correct to say that, by the end of the "first century Christianity became grafted onto conventional patterns of family life."[72] Thus did a certain branch of the church re-entrench itself into the Gentile patriarchal family structure, successfully resisting the implications of the gospel.

70. Browning, *Marriage and Modernization*, 165.

71. Ibid., 93.

72. MacDonald, "Was Celsus Right?," 175.

This is not to say that the ascetic branch or the gnostic branch were better embodiments of the family principle. Actually, *each* of the three branches represents a certain failure to hear Jesus and a resort to religious instincts that existed before Jesus: either the instinct for self-consciously pure religiosity (the ascetic branch), the instinct for social orderliness (the Pastoral branch), or the instinct for knowledge and independence (the gnostics). Neither asceticism, patriarchy, nor feelings of intellectual superiority really embodies Jesus' teachings. Each involves a self-righteous kind of spirituality; each assimilates Jesus' teachings to existing religious approaches. The message about the dignity of children got lost in the shuffle of the early struggles, from which the Pastoral branch emerged victorious.

It was inevitable that the teachings of Jesus would be partly obscured by the people who received, assimilated, and adapted his teachings, but these people *preserved* (partially) as well as *adapted* (wholly). Maybe the unconscious motto of religious organizations is "No preservation without assimilation!" What they do preserve for us is the reputation of Jesus as sage, prophet, healer, and friend of children, who also used the child as an image of the ideal believer. All of this contributed to a changed appreciation of children. Jesus' valuation of children goes hand in hand with his appreciation of the spiritual significance of the individual. He would often stop his sermons to minister to needy individuals. The gospel is a response to, and a rebuke of, the tendency to rank people by their perceived social status or usefulness. It has profound revolutionary implications and leads to social change not through political revolution but by "grass roots" changes that take place when people's attitudes are changed and their personal ethics are transformed.[73] This creates change from the bottom up, something more irresistible and long-lasting than partisan revolutions.

Slaves

Slaves are another category in the household that can be examined, that will simultaneously reveal the radicalism of Paul and the conservatism of the winning party among his successors. We have a priceless piece of very early evidence in Paul's letter to the slave-owning Christian, Philemon. Writing from prison, Paul admonishes Philemon to receive back his runaway slave Onesimus ("that is, my own heart," Phlm 12) with forgiveness ("welcome him as you would welcome me," 17). He strongly hints at something that

---

73. Greer, *Broken Lights and Mended Lives*, 101.

Philemon's Christian values should impel him to do, but he wants nothing "without your consent"; Philemon's decision must be "voluntary and not something forced" (14). The hint is that Philemon should free Onesimus, "so that you might have him back forever, no longer as a slave but more than a slave, a beloved brother" (15–16). Having led Philemon to the gospel, Paul is his spiritual patron, and he certainly could "command you to do your duty" (8), to "say nothing about your owing me even your own self" (19), but "I would rather appeal to you on the basis of love" (9). Knowing the power of a patron over a client, as well as the effectiveness of applying moral pressure with just the right amount of restraint, Paul feels confident "that you will do even more than I say" (21).

Paul skillfully praises Philemon and his family for their love, which has "refreshed" others (4–7), right before boldly referring to Philemon's duty (8) and reminding Philemon that he, Paul, is "a prisoner of Christ Jesus" (9). He slathers honey onto the underlying vinegar, making for an appeal that is hardly delicious but that might be irresistible. It is clever and careful but not actually subtle, at least not to someone who lived in a Hellenistic culture. It would be very clear that the patron (Paul) was demanding that a client (Philemon) grant something to another client (Onesimus). There are, however, two reasons why Paul must be careful in his rhetoric: Philemon does have legal rights over Onesimus, and Paul would have difficulty retaliating against a disobedient client under the circumstances.

Stepping back and looking at the bigger issue of exactly how the gospel could result in social change, we can best appreciate this if we understand these dynamics within society. Unlike in our time, people did not think in terms of idealized individual rights. Rights were situated within a network of relationships. We will fail to appreciate the enormity of the Christian ethical transformations if we insist on looking only for institutional political change—in fact, *immediate* political change. The changes Christianity introduced were not overt and political, but domestic and interpersonal. Contemplate the fact that Onesimus is really a new man with a new social status if he is "no longer as a slave but . . . a beloved brother"; he would truly be "more to you" than before, "both in the flesh and in the Lord" (16). To be "more . . . in the flesh" refers to social status, hinting at the need to free Onesimus.

If the moral pressure of Paul's method had not been compromised by the conservative successors of Paul, slavery would have been undone within a hundred years, but there was instead a compromise with the prevailing patriarchal household structure, and the only effect was a certain softening of the rules. The Hellenistic social system was built upon slavery, and many of the new converts were slaveholders. In the ensuing centuries, however, we see increasing Christian pressure to free slaves or to let them buy their freedom.[74]

Confucianism

There may be some value in comparing Christianity's family ethic to the strong emphasis upon loyalties within the family in the Confucian tradition. Further, it will give us an opportunity to see why theology is useful in the development of family ethics.

Confucianism, throughout the ages, always "argued for the irreducible role of the family in the generation of" values and that "if a person could not be a proper wife or husband, father or mother, parent or child, brother or sister," one could not be a "moral agent in the larger world."[75] Crucial values of reciprocity, deference, and self-discipline were learned in the family. This doctrine is profoundly optimistic, but also practical, about human nature. *Ren* is the inherent virtue of humanity;[76] *T'ien-ming* is the Mandate of Heaven that provides the model for human values; *Hsin* is human intelligence, which is inclined toward the moral life.[77]

Confucius did allow a concept of *Shang-Ti*, the "Lord on High,"[78] but this faded over time.[79] Confucianism had a ritual system, but it was weak in theology (teachings about divinity or God), and it has mostly ceased to be an active religion while persisting as a broad system of values and customs that still shape family life throughout the Far East, even in China, sixty years after a revolution that attempted to debunk and reject Confucian values as reactionary.[80]

74. Troeltsch, *Social Teaching of the Christian Churches*, 133.

75. Berthrong, *All Under Heaven*, 75.

76. What used to be transliterated "*jen*" is now transliterated "*ren*." The radical Mo made it mean "universal love," while the conservative Mencius understood it as benevolence (Van Norden, "Introduction," 20).

77. Berthrong, *All Under Heaven*, 73.

78. Viladesau and Massa, *World Religions*, 118 n. 1. Van Norden affirms that this was "originally a high deity" ("Introduction," 27).

79. Louden claims Confucius *was* religious. Truth depended on "something bigger than human nature," that was "outside of us," and was felt to be "sacred" (Louden, "'What Does Heaven Say?,'" 81).

80. In 1978 Deng Xiaoping brought China back from a farming disaster by

In Confucianism, we are not observing a family *metaphor* but a placing of family loyalties at the center of religious and social loyalties and philosophy. In fact, this is precisely Confucianism's greatest flaw: family became tyrannical;[81] the individual was suppressed. There was nothing to which family was secondary; it was part of a series of demanding and highly structured political loyalties. The irony of a family-centered religion is that it makes the family authoritarian and inflexible. A wife should always be subservient. As one saying had it, "if married to a rooster a woman should follow the rooster, and if married to a dog she should follow the dog."[82] Confucius himself should not be blamed for such an inhumane notion, but it is probably inevitable that such an expression would emerge in Confucian societies. Chinese Americans are finding that Western ideas of human rights are challenging the ancient "patriarchalism, clannishness, and group-over-individual viewpoint."[83] And, of course, Western ideas of the value of the individual draw heavily upon the teaching of Jesus (more joy in heaven over *one* repenting than over ninety-nine not needing to repent, etc.).

The only way to make family a supreme value while being able to critique it is to place it secondary to religious values, to see the family as based upon a higher pattern, and family loyalties as measurable by a higher standard. "Every family . . . takes its name" from the heavenly Father (Eph 3:15). We might still use the term "family" for that higher pattern ("the family of God"), but we are drawing upon transcendent values, which is the only way to avoid the tyranny of family. There must be values by which family can be continuously critiqued and improved.

---

reinstituting a version of Mencius's land reform program (Bell, *Beyond Liberal Democracy*, 241, 251).

81. Confucian values contribute to abusive situations in Korean families, according to Song, *Battered Women*, 3, 14, 40.

82. Yao, *Introduction to Confucianism*, 183.

83. Meyer, "Confucian 'Familism' in America," 181.

FIVE

"The two shall become one flesh"

The Evolution of Marriage

I MUST BEGIN WITH a return to the basics of the gospel, as taught and embodied by Jesus, and approach marriage only after having laid a groundwork in gospel. Marriage suggests family, and Jesus pictures relationships with God and with others as family relationships.

A Theology of the Child

Christian theologies often have been shamefully indifferent to the spiritual importance of the child. Authors may write about the "other" and the "marginalized" and completely ignore children. Theology needs to return to Jesus' own action, when he "took a little child and put it among them" (Mark 9:36), and when he said "it is to such as these that the kingdom of heaven belongs" (Matt 19:14). It belongs to *actual* children, and to adults who have not lost the honesty and teachability of children. Adrian Thatcher argues for a child-centered theology, one that values actual children as well as the quality of openness that children embody, and which adults are in danger of losing.[1] I think the premier childlike quality that Jesus is highlighting is teachability: willingness to learn something new.

Children cannot be excluded from the presence of Jesus and should not be excluded from theologies about Jesus. It is astonishing that so much theology has ignored Jesus' clearly stated solidarity of himself and of God with children: "Whoever welcomes one such child in my name welcomes me, and whoever welcomes me welcomes not me but the one who sent me"

---

1. Thatcher, *Theology and Families*, 59–60.

(Mark 9:37). Such "identity between Jesus and children" and such remarks as "Whoever wants to be first must be last of all and servant of all" (Mark 9:35), demonstrate a "radical, anti-hierarchical, power reversal taught by Jesus."[2]

Scripture preserves a clear picture of Jesus' valuation of children and of his radically ethical teaching. But Scripture also preserves the Household Codes, which are throwbacks to authoritarian and patriarchal structures in which *control* is the main issue; children must be "submissive and respectful in every way" (1 Tim 3:4). Thatcher argues that if we would have a theology that values children and manifests Christlike ethics, we must recognize that the primary revelation of God is not Scripture but Christ: "God's revelation in Christ must be given priority over God's revelation in scripture. . . . the love commandments of Jesus take priority over Household Codes. . . . All ethical practice is subject to revision as the church reflects further on the love commandments of Jesus."[3]

I affirm these findings. The revelation is *Jesus.* The New Testament writes *about* the revelation of God in the life and person of Jesus. The New Testament testifies to God and Christ, not to itself: "God . . . has shone in our hearts to give the light of the knowledge of the glory of God in the face of Jesus Christ" (2 Cor 4:6). The revelation of God is in the "face" or "person" (the Greek word *prosōpon* can mean either) of Christ. We need to continually return to Christ, with the help of his Spirit that guides us into all truth, so that we may continually rediscover the truth of love.

Truth is not frozen, but liquid. It shapes itself to answer the needs of the individual, the group, the age. This does not mean that truth is relativistic, but that it is *dynamic.* Our ethics must respond to our day and age. To express the Jesus-attitude in changed conditions requires a continual reshaping of ethics. Unless we continually rediscover Jesus' spirit and intention, we tend to slip into self-serving moralistic formulations. The values and the spirit of Jesus empower us to make new ethical discoveries and social adjustments. Society has not remained unchanged over the last two thousand years, so ethics cannot either.

The pace of change in recent generations, however, has put a great strain upon the social fabric. In the US today there is a severe gulf between conservatives and liberals, both in government and in the churches. Most debate takes the form of slogans; it is not "conversation" at all. Ultimately

2. Ibid., 61.
3. Ibid., 44–46.

the disputes are "about who gets to define the faith . . . They are disputes about how to read the Bible."[4]

Just as early Christians had to defend their differing understandings of the role of Jewish law, so do today's Christians need to defend (but often fail to do so!) their understanding of the role of the Scriptures, and of how church practice and thinking can legitimately undergo change. Most Protestant churches have women ministers now, in defiance of 1 Tim 2:12, but are they able to articulate the philosophy of biblical interpretation that enables them to no longer follow such verses? Preachers need to draw the congregation into a discussion of the various options for understanding changing church practice. Christians need to be more articulate about Bible, spiritual values, and culture.

Marriage Debates

The diversity of views about marriage today is likely to persist. There is no chance of one view becoming dominant and suppressing all other views. It would be impossible to impose uniformity on Christianity today. It is to be hoped that the teachings of Jesus will provide some unity that can prevent diversity from becoming destructively divisive.

The meaning of marriage has been undergoing progressive change for hundreds of years. From the time of the French troubadours[5] to the present, there has been a continuous heightening of the element of personal love, with a diminishing (not a disappearance) of the elements of interfamily alliance and social prestige. Much literature was written on the call of love being pitted against heartless social barriers and family selfishness. *Romeo and Juliet* is only the most famous of these writings.

Marriage historically meant the political and economic alliance of two families, and the creation of an heir was a primary purpose, but these have become secondary features. Marriage is now primarily understood as a love-commitment between two adults. Inasmuch as love is now understood as the main purpose of marriage, there is no longer any reason to admit only heterosexual, and to exclude homosexual, pairings from marriage. Marriage was the institution for the reception and raising of children, but the same biological and technological conditions no longer hold;

4. Jordan, *Blessing Same-Sex Unions*, 14.

5. Their romantic ideas developed apart from marriage, but the marriage institution soon adapted these notions, giving us highly romantic notions of marriage.

it is possible for homosexual couples to have children or to raise children originating in heterosexual pairings. Of course, gays will always be a small minority among the parents of any generation.

Social scientific findings indicate that a committed gay parental pair is comparable in many ways to a committed heterosexual pair. There is no basis for the fear that gay parents will turn the children gay. A study examining eighty-two boys who were parented by a gay couple found that "more than 90% of sons whose sexual orientations could be rated were heterosexual,"[6] about the same rate as in the general population. Another study found that "gay fathers were no different from nongay fathers in the overall intimacy factor" with their children but were strongly motivated "to be 'better' fathers" due to "stronger feelings of guilt about their role in fathering children" and sensitivity to being scrutinized by society; they also tended to exercise more authority over their children.[7] There is no scientific basis to the fear that gay marriage will destroy the family or society. The evidence speaks of conscientious parenting by gays.

The debate around same-sex marriage is highly polarized and often characterized by ill will. Each side seems to be unable to comprehend the values of the other and to assume bad motivation by the other. We need to notice is that this is a debate among Christians. And we need to notice when we are using (and blending) different ethical systems. Rights-based ethical systems may be the dominant in the West today. Jewish and Christian ethics have assumed a God who revealed his will in Scripture and who designated the committed relationship between one man and one woman (despite the polygamous traditions associated with the patriarchs) as providing the right environment into which children would be born and raised. Psychological and social studies confirm that this arrangement is better for children than single-parent homes, even when the single parent has the best of intentions. That raises another standard of ethics: psychological health and social functionality, one that can profitably be put into conversation with biblical thought.

It was not so long ago that Christianity frowned upon sex itself and only grudgingly tolerated even married sex for purposes of procreation. Sex for pleasure was considered either immoderate or sinful by saintly moralizers like Augustine. Condemnations of sexual pleasure have largely been dropped, leaving the ban on same-sex love as the last bastion of Christian

6. Bailey et al, "Sexual Orientation of Adult Sons," 124 (the abstract).

7. Bigner and Jacobsen, "Parenting Behaviors," 181.

moralism ("moralism" being the term for self-righteous and intellectually shallow forms of moral commentary). It is necessary and inevitable that institutions, including marriage, evolve. Glaser argues that, "Just as Jesus declared the institution of the Sabbath was made for humanity . . . so marriage is made for us, not we for the institution of marriage."[8]

One of the arguments that has been used against homosexuality is that it does not issue in children. But the fact that marriage is no longer based on procreative issues is shown by the allowance of non-procreative marriages between older men and women. Since the main motive for marrying is now understood to be love, there does not seem to be any compelling reason for forbidding a loving and committed marriage between two people of the same sex.

In the first edition of this book, I said that marriage was the institution for the bearing of children and that a new institution was needed for committed gay relationships.[9] Within a week of that book going to press, I realized I had changed my mind. I now think that the institution for committed gay relationships already exists. It is called marriage. The new institution that is needed (or rather the new category *within* marriage) is for the raising of children. Marriage law in the US tends to focus on *rights*: insurance, inheritance, and parental rights. In recent decades, many judges have rightfully been emphasizing the needs of children over the rights of adults. Attention to the needs of children signals the beginning of a sea change in spirituality, but the tide still has quite a way to rise.

The child-bearing institution (or category *within* the institution of marriage) will need to be more focused on *responsibilities* than on rights, and more focused on children than on parents. Ideally, child-bearing should be a status for which couples must qualify, and in which they must receive some training, but this is hard to imagine without the acceptance of a new set of values, one that puts the needs of children first. Institutions of parental counseling and training need to arise within faith communities. Ministers should be more rigorous in their marriage counseling practices, and should refuse to conduct marriages that they deem unlikely to endure. High rates of divorce are due to the loose standards of ministers, as much as to the loose morals of the people entering the marriage. The same standards of seriousness about fidelity and commitment should be applied, whether the applicants for marriage are gay or straight.

8. Glaser, *As My Own Soul*, 59.
9. Finlan, *Family Metaphor* (first edition), 88.

Forcing gay couples into a different legal category ("civil unions" and the like) will inevitably be an avenue for the surreptitious reintroduction of prejudice. Supposed defenders of the family who think that homosexuals are a threat to the family are expressing fear and manifesting psychological fragility. The main threat to marriages has always been irresponsible and selfish behavior by the marital pair. Further, it is the ingracious and prejudicial attitude of some heterosexuals that radicalizes many homosexuals. Perhaps what is most frightening is having to *discuss* love and culture with people who are not convinced by quotations from Leviticus or Romans.[10] What is scary, perhaps, is having to explain one's beliefs, but that is a requirement for any mature Christian. Mere conformity to prevailing social attitudes and prejudices is sub-Christian. We should be able to explain our values, and say why we favor some Bible passages over others.

Caving In or Piling On?

Many Christians oppose recommendations such as these on the grounds that this would be caving in to secular society. This is based on the belief (the *myth*) that true biblical believers do not give in to changes going on in secular culture. But this conveniently overlooks the many ways that believers *already* accommodate themselves to secular culture: cooperating with systems of usury, including credit cards (*contra* Neh 5:7–10); withholding a worker's wages beyond nightfall (*contra* Deut 24:15); wearing makeup and jewelry (*contra* Isa 3:16–23); and holding to a form of government not found in the Bible (democracy).

The antiquity of certain fears and hostilities is no justification for their perpetuation. Cruelty is the sign of a diseased society and not to be defended by those who would stand for the Master's teaching. There is no longer any good reason for excluding responsible gay people from any position of responsibility or leadership in the church. Of course, all leaders need to be held accountable, and there must be sensible cautions and controls whenever supervision of young people is involved, but this is equally true of heterosexual leaders.

Homosexuals should not be treated as convenient scapegoats or wicked social pariahs. It is only the cowardice of narrow-minded conformists that slanders homosexuals as a threat to the family. It is the addictive and

10. The most commonly cited anti-homosexual passages are Lev 18:22; 20:13; Rom 1:26–27.

unregenerate behavior of one or both parents that threatens any *individual* family, and thus the abstract "family." What breaks up any family? Parental bickering, sexual infidelity, patterns of abuse or victimization, and the addictive or immature behavior of the parental pair. The attempt to vilify homosexuality as the cause of family breakdown is a cowardly move designed to divert attention from the disordered behavior of irresponsible parents.

Commitments in Any Marriage

The need to counsel young couples before marriage exists whether the couple is heterosexual or homosexual. The need to have mature, committed individuals enter into marriage with adult thoughtfulness and foresight and with a promise of fidelity, holds true whether the couple is gay or straight. When *desire* is taken as a sufficient criterion for marriage, the frequency of divorce will be high. When compatibility of loyalties and interests is taken seriously, marriage success becomes more likely.

We cannot ignore the fact that stable and secure married life is good for children; numerous studies confirm this.[11] Furthermore, marriage is good for men: "A society of families both constrains male aggression and channels them toward the protection and support of family."[12] This also is true of gay men, even though the author of the previous quotation would not approve. As Thatcher argues, the "marital values" of "deepening love, life-long fidelity, and mutual commitment" are what really matter in any family, and these are a reflection of "an icon of the Triune God who is Love."[13] Such marital values can be reflected in non-married relationships, and also in same-sex relationships.[14]

Wherever the values of love and loyalty are lived out in a long-term commitment, *there* is true marriage. Wherever there is infidelity, cruelty, dishonesty, there is no marriage worthy of the name. The key criteria are the seriousness, the devotion, and the values of the pair entering into marriage. Pastors should not perform any marriage where the pair has not been counseled and questioned about these matters. Hasty or thoughtless marriages, gay or straight, are destined to fail.

11. For instance Morgan, *Farewell to the Family?*; Thatcher, *Theology and Families*, 120–24.

12. Gilder, *Men and Marriage*, 111.

13. Thatcher, *Theology and Families*, 134–35.

14. Ibid., 135–37.

A trinitarian theology of family can unify ancient beliefs with modern insights. If one reflects on father, mother, and child in light of trinitarian theology, one finds that gender fades away. Trinitarian theology highlights intimacy and relationships; the Father and the Mother-Son together generate the Spirit, who corresponds to child. The equality of the persons of the Trinity implies a high value for the child in the family.[15]

15. This builds on Thatcher, *Theology and Families*, 173–74, 181, 183, 185–86, though Thatcher does not use the term "Mother-Son."

SIX

"Mercy, not sacrifice"

Religious Priorities

THE USE OF FAMILY metaphors for God and for believers by Jesus and Paul conveys the values of intimacy, love, trust, and mutual support. A loving father encourages the growth of sons and daughters, while brothers and sisters will support each other. A parental God suggests a different set of values than God as stern judge or as unapproachable Holy One. This chapter will seek to unfold the fundamental values and priorities that Jesus means to communicate. The focus will be on meaning-content rather than on the metaphor-vehicle. But first we must ask some questions about the strangeness of *religions*.

Why is it that religions seem to evolve so slowly and to perpetuate so much superstition and hostility to other religions? It is partly the fact that religion is always deeply involved in the values and traditions of particular groups, and so with the defining of social boundaries and the rejection of out-groups and out-group characteristics as a function of group survival. But there is more, having to do with the boundaries of human consciousness, which makes religion the arena for the deep, the delusional, the imaginary, and the uncertain.

Religion often explores the marginal, the outrageous, the horrifying, the unbearable, the unreachable. But these explorations are not always healthy. They express everything that is in the religious heart: fear, imagination, desire for prestige, quest for meaning, the impulse to escape, truth-hunger, moral insight, spiritual hope, intimations of immortality.

Religion is a storehouse of good and evil, of maturation and of failure to mature, of vision and of obsession. But the religious life of Jesus shows an instinct for moral unification and love, based on trust in the watchcare of the heavenly Father. We see the sanity of Jesus in all his interactions with people, his impatience with pompous and unloving teachers, his outrage with hypocrites, and his gentleness with people who had been wounded by life, even if they were not ideal models of family life—the woman at the well (John 4:7–27), the woman caught in adultery (John 8:1–11), the blind beggar (Mark 10:46–52), the woman who anointed his feet (Luke 7:37–48). Jesus' revelation is not just his teachings but his life of trust and familiarity with God, which led to a life with others that was devoid of fear and coercion. "Do not be afraid" was virtually the watchword of his religious life—a religion without psychopathology.

Spiritual Need

But let us not leave psychopathology behind quite yet! We need to observe that all of us who had any serious relationship problems with our parents will certainly import them into our relationship with God. We expect arbitrariness, cruelty, and severity from God only if we experienced these things as children. If we learned certain defensive skills for dealing with temperamental parents, we will use them in our later religious life: bargaining with God, concealing our feelings from God, or appeasing God by undergoing suffering or penance. It has long been common for people to bring into their relationship with God their deeply ingrained concepts of *payment through suffering*. Life is purgatory for many Christians.

Obviously, then, the Father metaphor is not a cure-all for religious problems. In fact it can actually help to bring out the patterns of fear and the extreme coping strategies that we learned at an early age. Calling God "Father" can actually help us become aware of our emotional injuries, and Jesus knew he would have to become the Great Physician for many injured souls. He wanted to make it easy for people to seek healing from him, and this meant fighting off the self-righteous critics who frowned on the needy people who came to him. This afforded him the opportunity to affirm neediness, and to contrast it with self-righteousness: "Those who are well have no need of a physician, but those who are sick. . . . For I have come to call not the righteous but sinners" (Matt 9:12–13). He is defending those who *know* they need a physician or who *know* they are sinners.

In times past, people had a sharp conscious of sin; today, we have a sharper awareness of our sickness or woundedness. Jesus opens the door to both kinds of needy people at the same time. Having a consciousness either of one's illness or one's wrongdoing seems to be an entry requirement. An awareness of *need* is necessary to receiving any help from Jesus. Only those who *know* they need healing can receive it.

This Matthew 9 passage is also where Jesus makes a sharp contrast between two types of religious motivation, the moral or spiritual kind ("mercy") and the ritual or purity-obsessed kind ("sacrifice"), quoting the prophet Hosea to make his point. In Hosea's Hebrew, God says "I desire steadfast love [*chesed*] and not sacrifice, the knowledge of God rather than burnt offerings" (6:6). *Chesed* is one of the richest Hebrew words, meaning loyalty, love, solidarity within a family, or kindness (the latter in Gen 20:13; Ruth 2:20).[1] The New Testament, of course, is written in Greek. The word used where Jesus quotes Hos 6:6 is *eleos*, meaning "mercy" (as in Matt 12:7), compassion, love. Jesus is in sync with Hosea, who is definitely setting moral motives in opposition to the cultic approach,[2] just as Isaiah's God disdains "the blood of bulls" in place of doing good and seeking justice (Isa 1:17), and as Micah mocks the extravagance of "thousands of rams" and even child sacrifice, in place of what God really wants of us—"to do justice, and to love kindness, and to walk humbly with your God" (Mic 6:6–8).[3] Jeremiah says God commanded obedience, *not* sacrifice, from the Exodus generation (Jer 7:22–23; Amos makes a similar point in 5:21–25).[4]

Jesus is in line with these prophets in exalting the higher loyalties of religion over mere ritual and social propriety. The Pharisees had just criticized him for eating with "tax collectors and sinners" (Matt 9:11), and he gives a dual answer: one needs to learn about the values and attributes of God ("mercy") rather than being concerned about ritual purity and one needs to have an awareness of one's own spiritual need. So: "Go and learn what this means, 'I desire mercy, not sacrifice.' For I have come to call not the righteous but sinners" (9:13).

---

1. The "ch" is an aspirated "k" sound, as in "Bach," not as our usual English "ch" sound.

2. God rejects the priests (Hos 4:6–9) and their "altars for sinning" (8:11–14). Making altars seems to go with greed and violence (10:1–8; 6:6–9; 12:8–11).

3. The psalmist also mocks the idea of God needing to eat bulls and goats (Ps 50:12–13; cf. 40:6).

4. Scholars often downplay the sharpness of these attacks on priestly religion. And, of course, not all prophets are the same. Malachi, Joel, and Ezekiel have a strong interest in sacrifice. Sacrifice is *linked* to, not *contrasted* with, right-doing in Ps 4:5; Deut 33:19; Mal 1:13; but other prophets saw cult as blinding people to the real values of the covenant (Hendel, "Prophets, Priests," 189–97).

Why are these two different points being made at the same time? They turn out to be deeply linked at the level of fundamental values (matters of "ultimate concern," to use Tillich's phrase).[5] Alignment with highest values (mercy, love, loyalty to God) requires that that these values always be placed above any ritual considerations and also requires that we seek spiritual healing, because if we deny that we are spiritually ill, we act out of arrogance and a judgmental attitude. We humans have more aggression than we admit (an insight both of moral religion and of psychology). We see the speck in the eye of another but don't notice the log in our own (Matt 7:3); we cleanse our hands but not our actions (Matt 15:19–20).

Fastidious self-righteousness and meticulous observance of ritual go together; both manifest a failure to discern the higher values.[6] True values will always illuminate a way toward spiritual healing and character transformation. "The weightier matters of the law: justice and mercy and faith" are the only preventive for spiritual blindness, excessive concern for cleansing "the outside of the cup" to the neglect of the "inside of the cup" (Matt 23:23–28).

Ritual correctness is often a cover-up for ethical insensitivity and spiritual blindness, and we see this illustrated in the other place in Matthew where Jesus quotes Hos 6:6. In Matthew 12, the Pharisees confront Jesus for allowing his disciples to glean from the fields on the Sabbath. It is not an accusation of theft but of a ritual violation (working on the Sabbath).

Jesus links the Pharisees' hostility and blindness (their ethical and cognitive shortcomings) to their ritualism (their religious-conceptual shortcoming). He says "if you had known what this means, 'I desire mercy and not sacrifice,' you would not have condemned the guiltless" (Matt 12:7). It is *because* of their obsession with ritual correctness that they are indifferent to human need, blind to the mission of Jesus, and condemn the innocent. He equates the situation with that of David "when he and his companions were hungry," who entered the temple and "ate the bread of the Presence," which is meant only for the priests; doing their Sabbath work, "the priests break the sabbath and yet are guiltless" (Matt 12:3–5; 1 Sam 21:2–7). There are at least four implications of this comparison: that human need should take priority over ritual fastidiousness, that holy work can break ritual restrictions, that Jesus is like a new David, and that his followers are like priests.

5. Tillich, *Dynamics of Faith*, 1–4, 88–91.

6. In terms of Fowler's stages, this could be described as an insight of the higher stages (4 to 6) when looking upon the relatively shallow and conformist religious life of Stage 3.

There is a heavy messianic hint here, as well as an emphasis on ethics. Jesus is a new David, his followers have physical need, and they are doing holy work (like priests).

It takes us a while to see the connection that is crystal-clear to Jesus, between religious priorities (either mercy or ritual) and ethical behavior (either just or unjust). He is saying that if we understood Hosea, we would be just, sensitive to human need, reverent of holy work, respectful of innocence, and would recognize the Messiah! All this in a few verses.

I have chosen Matthew because it is the only one with the Hosea quote, which provides the ethical basis (mercy not ritual ["sacrifice"]) for what Jesus says in all three Synoptic versions of this story. Mark makes the same point in a different way, with a radical saying that sounds like the pronouncement of a spiritual law: "the sabbath was made for humankind, not humankind for the sabbath" (Mark 2:27).[7] As in Matthew, the message here is that humans are more important than ritual institutions. Luke, usually very strong on moral points, lacks either of these verses. All three Synoptics have the same climactic remark, "The Son of Man is lord of the Sabbath" (Matt 12:8; Luke 6:5; Mark 2:28). In Matthew and Mark, it comes right after the ethical point (about mercy or about humankind), so it seems to mean that humanity ("Son of Man") is more important than ritual ("Sabbath"). In Semitic languages, "son of X" means "having the nature of X," so "son of Man" can mean "mortal, human." Ezekiel uses "son of man" this way (2:1; 3:3; etc.). Jesus' point would be that humanity matters more than the ritual (Sabbath); the ritual should be in service to humanity, not the other way around.

But there is also likely an eschatological meaning. Jesus calls himself "the Son of Man" in the Gospels, and "Son of Man" was an eschatological figure in found in Dan 7:13 and in the Similitudes of Enoch (within *1 Enoch*). The Son of Man in Daniel will be given a kingdom and will judge the nations. The heavenly Son of Man figure in *1 Enoch*, on the other hand, is a pre-existent divine figure "to whom belongs righteousness," who "is the light of gentiles and he . . . has revealed the wisdom of the Lord of the Spirits to . . . the holy ones" (*1 Enoch* 46:3; 48:4, 7).[8] The Son of Man in *1 Enoch* existed "before the creation of the stars" (48:3; cf. 48:6; 62:7). He is

---

7. In this case, the NRSV is not just being politically correct in choosing "humankind." The Greek is *anthrōpos*, which is grammatically masculine but can mean either "man" or "human being." There is a word for a specifically masculine person: *anēr*.

8. Translations are by E. Isaac in the standard work in the field, *The Old Testament Pseudepigrapha*, edited by James H. Charlesworth. This quotation is from vol. 1, p. 35.

"the prototype of the Before-Time" (46:2). "He shall proclaim peace to you in the name of the world that is to become. For from here proceeds peace since the creation of the world" (71:15).

1 Enoch's Son of Man passages emphasize divinity and pre-existence. There is judgment throughout *1 Enoch*, but in the Son of Man passages, judgment is not directed against Gentiles, but against "sinners" (46:4; 62:2), and there is more emphasis on positive fate in the afterlife: "All the elect ones shall stand before him" (62:9); "All evil shall disappear from before his face" (69:29). Due to the absence of these middle chapters from the copies of *1 Enoch* found at Qumran, we cannot know whether Jesus knew of them, but his values certainly resonate with those of the Enochian Son of Man: "he will become the hope of those who are sick in their hearts" (*1 Enoch* 48:4). The "Son of Man" in the Gospels seems to picture Jesus as a sort of heavenly Messiah and light of the Gentiles.[9] All three Synoptics affirm that he has more authority than the Sabbath. The "lord of the Sabbath" statement is in the climactic position in Luke's version. In Mark and Matthew, the climax is shared by some anti-ritual principles.

Both the ethical and the messianic meanings of "lord of the Sabbath" are probably intended, as they flow perfectly well from what precedes. The ethical point is established in the preceding verse (Matt 12:7; Mark 2:27); the messianic point is made earlier (Jesus as David, his followers as priests). The ethical meaning is the most obvious, and could not have been missed by anyone; this point could be paraphrased, "my followers are hungry; leave them alone; they are doing holy work; people are more important than ritual rules anyway." The messianic point is more subtle, which fits with Jesus' approach to this thorny issue throughout his career. Sometimes he uses "Son of Man" to speak about what any mortal must go through, sometimes to speak about what he himself is up to. Do we have to assume that Mark invented this clever convergence of ethics and Christology, or that Matthew drew these meanings out of Hos 6:6? Was not Jesus clever enough to use a prophet to strengthen his ethical point or to make a statement with both ethical and messianic meaning? He is a Messiah who will bring spiritual revelation and ethical consciousness.

Whether one comes in through the front door (through the truth to the Messiah) or through the back door (through the Messiah to the truth), the result is the same, and his sheep will know his voice.

9. Matt 8:10–12; 24:27–31; Luke 2:32; 9:26; 12:8; see also John 17:5.

The two usages of Hos 6:6 in Matthew alert us to deep interconnections between religious concepts and ethical practice. In Matt 9:13, Jesus validates spiritual neediness and affirms God's preference for mercy over ritual purity. (To have mercy is to care about the spiritually needy.) In 12:7–8, Jesus also validates human need (hunger) over ritual rules, affirms his Messiahship, and traces his enemies' injustice (condemning the guiltless) to their incomprehension of the Hosea principle.

Politics of Religion

In the next story Jesus heals a man's deformed hand on the Sabbath, and "the Pharisees went out and conspired against him" (Matt 12:9–14).[10] This epitomizes the spiritual blindness of superficially religious people. To put it in terms of Fowler's stages, it shows how stubborn and cruel people can be when they refuse to advance beyond Stage 3—conventional and conformist religion, honoring God only "with their lips" (Mark 7:6). To put it in moral terms, when religious leaders are desperate to hold on to power, they will betray any principle, commit any wrong. This is really politics, not (genuine) religion. It has nothing to do with God.

It is this common phenomenon of political selfishness and plotting that is one of the strongest arguments against religious organizations getting involved in political reform movements. Let religion supply the motivation and the values, but let the church stay out of political alliances and lobbying for political programs. It is a recipe for division in the church (between liberal and conservative) and for the rise of narcissistic opportunists within the church.

When liberation theologians claim that the biblical message was always political, was "not the proclamation of a universal God to a universal humanity, but a particular message to a particular human community,"[11] they are taking us back to a time before Jesus, ignoring the changes he

10. It is politically correct now to deny any historical accuracy to the blame attaching to the Pharisees, but the scenario given in the Gospels is entirely plausible. Having tremendous power in the towns and cities of Galilee and Judaea, the Pharisees would have had to either support or oppose a prophet and healer operating in those towns. If they wanted him arrested, they would have needed the help of the Sadducees (who had the power in Jerusalem). How *often* have clerical leaders (*especially* Christian ones!) conspired against independent teachers?

11. Ferm, *Contemporary American Theologies*, 68, summarizing the view of Juan Luis Segundo.

brought. Jesus demands that we progress beyond the national stage of human development and thinking, that we notice the goodness in the despised Samaritan, that we be ready to encounter more faith in a Roman than in all Israel (see Luke 10:33; Matt 8:10). Does liberation theology fail to hear the imperative to transcend the tyranny of politics, to move beyond the isolation of group from group, class from class? The insistence on "particular communities" and classes even distorts the OT prophets, who were constantly universalizing the God-concept: "Many nations shall join themselves to the Lord on that day" (Zech 2:11). Is this a provincial God?—"Let the nations be glad and sing for joy, for you judge the peoples with equity and guide the nations upon earth" (Ps 67:4); "that my salvation may reach to the end of the earth" (Isa 49:6).

But even more is the NT a message to "universal humanity," and to lose that is to lose the gospel itself. God shows no favoritism. To favor any group is to betray the message to Jew and Greek, rich and poor, male and female (Gal 3:28). The religion of Jesus is liberal enough to allow each one to personally experience a unique walk with God, yet unifying enough to bring us together in one family and righteous enough to demand that we conquer our provincialism and selfishness.[12] To introduce his apostles to the new frontiers of the spiritual kingdom, Jesus took them on preaching tours outside of Judaea and Galilee, to Phoenicia and the Decapolis,[13] primarily Gentile areas.

When the church lobbies for *one* group, that is politics. The gospel is constantly asking groups to surrender their self-righteousness and be open to the *other*, the Samaritan. The "Samaritan" in any person's mentality may be rich or poor, black or white—whoever is politically vilified. Politicized religion is a return to the ages of provincialized identity. When politics and religion are blended, politics takes over and the religious spirit is suppressed, though religious language may persist, may even increase.

A Universalizing Force

Jesus proclaimed the availability of spiritual sonship and daughtership to all, thus presenting a religious approach that can be utilized in any age and at any level of culture. He did not make this message dependent upon one

12. John 11:52; Luke 2:32; Rom 10:12. Again are they amplifying the principles of the prophets: Mic 4:4–5; 6:8; Amos 9:7; Isa 19:23–25.

13. Mark 7:24, 31; Matt 15:21.

cultural condition or on arrangements in the empire, for cultures change and empires collapse. By teaching universal sonship, he set in motion the greatest universalizing force, in the wake of which many social changes can happen. Unfortunately, many of these social changes were preempted by the politics of an empire that began to see the political usefulness of Christianity. The universalizing trend was taken over by *imperial* universalizing. Compromises were made that enabled Christianity and empire to coexist. Christianity became a unifying influence in Western Europe, but this was nine parts natural and political for every part that was truly derived from Jesus. The false unity that was enforced by the sword under later emperors was not sponsored by our Lord. But Jesus has always lurked within Christianity, ready to break out like an armed force from a Trojan horse, endeavoring to reconquer the religion that took his name but betrayed his spirit.

The message of revelation tends to get diluted by social habit and mental inertia, while political self-interest does worse than dilute it. Man is social, and so must religion be, but religious idealism points out the *inwardness* of personality, changing society by changing the individual. Religious unity must be founded upon an enlightened concept of personality (the significance of each child of God) balanced with recognition of the unity of Deity (which is all-encompassing). Perfection without unity is a contradiction in terms, but unity does not mean conformity. It means a coordination of law and creativity, responsibility and freedom. This requires resistance to the tyranny of politics, on one side, or of the anarchy of individualism, on the other.

For we have one Father above all and in us all, and we are all brothers. There must be one fold and one shepherd, so that we can gather together in unity the scattered children of God, and all of us be transformed from one degree of glory into another, into the likeness of God, who is Spirit.[14]

A Father instead of a King

The upshot of this chapter has been that, for those who would follow Jesus, psychological health is inseparable from religious faith, advancing ethics, and progress in religious philosophy (including detaching the realm of God from the realm of Caesar). Jesus calls not only for trust in God, and not only for embodiment of steadfast love, but he wants his disciples to understand something about philosophic and spiritual progress, to make the necessary

14. Eph 4:6; Matt 23:8; John 10:16; 11:52; 2 Cor 3:18.

distinctions (mercy not sacrifice) and connections (the pure in heart will see God). Progress is in spiritual character and in religious conceptualization. Most of the religious concepts he offered were connected with the family image. Some relied on the already-existing kingdom of God image, but who is at the head of Jesus' "kingdom"? A Father. Who are members of this kingdom? Brothers and sisters (Mark 3:35; Matt 23:8–9). Following Jesus means penetrating past the *kingdom* image and seeing the *familial* values (intimacy, care, growth) that underlie Jesus' kingdom.

Undoubtedly, Jesus had to use the more familiar kingdom image in order to grab his audience's attention, at which point he insinuated the more spiritual idea. His kingdom parables rarely said anything about a king or subjects but constantly spoke of God's fatherly interest in the spiritual growth and qualities of his children—and God always notices these qualities: "your Father who sees in secret will reward you" (Matt 6:6). God notices who is sincere and who is pompous (Luke 18:9–14).

It certainly ought to strike us as anomalous that this is a kingdom with no *king*, but only a father. "Kingdom" resounded with ancient thinking and resonated with prophetic hopes, but "father" resounded with more tender values, which he illustrated with stories like the parable of the lost (or prodigal) son. It takes several readings to detect all the fascinating details in this apparently simple story. One that leaps out at any reader who is familiar with the norms of Middle Eastern families is the extraordinarily demonstrative love of the father. Unlike the typical Middle Eastern father, this one is forlorn over the departure of his young son and is watching and waiting for his return. For when the wayward son finally does return, "while he was still far off, his father saw him and was filled with compassion; he ran and put his arms around him and kissed him" (Luke 15:20). This is extraordinary and unseemly behavior for a Middle Eastern patriarch! Jesus is going out of his way to show that the father is exceptionally loving and cares nothing for status. Where a typical father from his part of the world would be stern and scolding with the returning son, this father embraces him immediately and hardly cares about the humble confession of unworthiness the son wants to make (v. 21). The father seems to interrupt him, calling to the servants to bring out the best robe and ring, and to cook up a calf, "let us eat and celebrate; for this son of mine was dead and is alive again" (vv. 23–24).

Nothing more is said about the prodigal; he had done his deed: repenting and humbly returning to his father. He needed to do nothing more than soak in the love he had missed. The other son suddenly became the antagonist. When he heard that the noisy celebration was for the return of his brother, "he became angry and refused to go in. His father came out and began to plead with him" (v. 28). *Pleading*! Here again we see the extraordinary effort this father will make to reach out to any son. Stories are made interesting by exaggerating certain characteristics, and in this case it is the father's demonstrative love.

So which one is truly the lost son? The prodigal "*was* lost and *is* found!" (v. 24). The last we hear of the other brother is his resentful complaint about a fatted calf being slaughtered for the wayward (prostitute-mongering!) son while he, the *good* boy, was never given even a young goat for a celebration (vv. 29–30). This is *really* the lost son, who dwells in his pride and wants to extract demonstrations of love from his father like payment from an employer. This son does not know his father's real nature. The answer has nothing to do with *deserving* but only with the father's gracious love—for *both* of his sons. He loves the self-righteous son as much as he loves the irresponsible one: "all that is mine is yours. But we had to celebrate and rejoice, because this brother of yours was dead and has come to life" (v. 31–32). The salvation of the lost one must be celebrated! Anything else is unthinkable. Joy is essential in this family.

As with many of Jesus' parables, some of the characters (the sons) are entirely selfish, but the story allows that even a selfish person can turn about and make a right decision, and the prodigal son does this. In the depth of his poverty and despair, he "came to himself" (Luke 15:17) and decided to humbly return to his father, admit his unworthiness, and seek to be received at a lower status ("like one of your hired hands" v. 19). Though selfish, he at least knows when to eat humble pie! It was the other brother, the self-righteous one, who did not know how to surrender his pride, who refused to join the celebration. Perhaps this is the only hell: to deliberately exclude oneself from the father's joy.

The father in the parable is completely inviting and wholly without narcissism. He restores the son without assigning blame, decreeing punishment, or even hearing a completed confession. He cares little about the son's confession—he just wants to celebrate! This is not a judge, nor a king, but rather a tenderhearted father. The envious brother does not understand this; he wants his father to favor him. But the father does not play favorites. He does not judge or put down either son but seeks reconciliation and joy at every turn. He is like the shepherd who won't abandon one sheep, even for the sake of ninety-nine; or the woman who searches diligently for one lost coin (Luke 15:3–10, immediately preceding the prodigal son story). God seeks out the lost, and "the Son of Man came to seek out and to save the lost" (Luke 19:10). God is even "kind to the ungrateful and the wicked" (Luke 6:35).

Most Christian theologies end up downplaying this teaching about the generosity of God. The most popular form of atonement theology has God functioning as a judge and a king more than as a father. Popular atonement theology assumes that a sacrifice has to be made, sin has to be punished, and proper order must be restored, since sin had shown dishonor to God.[15] Each one of these notions is refuted in the parable. The father does not act like an indignant judge or an offended king; he imposes no punishment, assigns no blame, and is not even remotely anxious about his honor. Traditional atonement advocates are, in fact, playing the role of the rigid-minded brother when they insist on blame, punishment, and honor. These attitudes are full of anxiety and defensiveness—and the father has none of that. Forgiveness imposes no sacrifice, payment, or demonstration of public humiliation—at least if we take Jesus' teaching seriously. Of course, the repentant one might feel the need to make reparations or to assume a humble profile, and this is a sensible reaction, but it is not imposed by the Father.

These two systems of thought simply cannot be reconciled: the loving parental attitude of the father in Jesus' teachings, and the idea of a father who would not forgive until he received sufficient sacrificial payment for human sin, a payment in blood, for which only *innocent* blood could suffice. The latter notion blends ancient concepts of ritual, magic, and retribution. It has nothing to do with forgiveness or with the attitude of a loving parent. There can be no blending of forgiveness with the notion of a payment in blood—and yet popular atonement doctrines attempt precisely this mixing of Jesus' teaching about the Father with ancient superstitions about a sacrifice-demanding deity. It is not surprising that the severe value systems of the ancient world should give rise to the latter idea, but we need to notice that it reflects the distorted thinking of generations of wounded children, grown into adults. But the Father of Jesus *does* offer forgiveness freely and does *not* exact torture, humiliation, or vengeance upon his children.

---

15. Anselm of Canterbury bases his atonement logic on this concept of sin as disorder and as insult against God's honor.

What Kind of Father?

To a large degree, children derive their concepts of God from the habits of attachment they develop in childhood. Healthy attachment patterns are to be distinguished from avoidant patterns (where the child learns to avoid the parents) and ambivalent patterns (where the child never knows whether the parent will be kind or cruel, rational or irrational). Secure attachment generates concepts of God as reliably loving "and present. Avoidant attachment with God involves construals of God as distant . . . Ambivalent attachment [generates] images of God as inconsistently available."[16] Looking at our historic concepts of God, we would have to say that they testify to a long history of hard knocks and traumatized thinking.

Nor can we blame Judaism and glorify Christianity in this regard. Christian theologians have often stressed the supposed necessity for violent punishment of sin, interpreting the death of Jesus as a vicarious bearing of divine wrath, a sacrificial payment for sin. Gregory the Great, Calvin, and many others built their theories upon metaphors of sacrifice in the epistles,[17] taking them very literally and reducing to secondary status the many teachings that link soteriology to simple trust, honesty, and doing good.[18] When atonement became the dominant soteriological paradigm, certain epistle passages became the lens through which the Gospels were read (and through which the epistles were read, as well).

But let us see what damage this has done to the concept of God. The notion that God *had* to punish someone for human sin but was willing to punish the one innocent person and so to overlook the sins of all the guilty people, undermines the concepts of both divine justice and forgiveness. It was not *forgiveness* if payment was required, and it was not *justice* if the innocent had to pay the price. This theology makes God either less than all-powerful (if he had no choice but *had* to find a sacrificial victim), less than just (able to be bribed), or less than sane (making forgiveness dependent on a ritual murder).

In contrast, Jesus reasoned that God can do whatever he wants; that he is truly just and loving; and that forgiveness is immediately available: "Friend, your sins are forgiven you" (Luke 5:20; cf. 7:48). Salvation is

16. Sandage, *Transforming Spirituality*, 182.

17. Rom 3:25; 4:25; 8:3; 1 Cor 5:7; 2 Cor 5:21; Heb 9:22–28; 1 Tim 2:6; 1 Pet 1:18–19; 1 John 2:2; 4:10.

18. Mark 3:33–35; 12:30–34; Matt 5:8; 7:8–10; 12:35–37; 25:34–40; Luke 6:45; 7:47–50; 8:48; 18:17; James 1:27; 4:8.

offered in the present moment, not as a reward for correct doctrine, but as a response to honest spiritual desire: "'According to your faith let it be done to you.' And their eyes were opened" (Matt 9:29–30). Seven times in the Synoptics we see Jesus saying, "your faith has made you well" or "has saved you,"[19] and never once does he tell the recipients of his saving power to believe anything about his coming death or teach any complicated substitutionary concept.

God is not an angry judge who needs a victim, nor a tribal deity who requires blood-sacrifice, nor an enraged and abusive father. Rather, "the Father himself loves you" (John 16:27). "Do not be afraid, little flock, for it is your Father's good pleasure to give you the kingdom" (Luke 12:32). Whenever Jesus used the image of God as Judge (that being what people understood), he always guided people back to the image of the intimate Father who does not want "one of these little ones [to] be lost" (Matt 18:14).

Are we saying there is no aspect of judgment or correction in God's parental attitude? No, but we do say that most concepts of God's judgment derive their content from human narcissism and desire for control. The image of an angry and petulant God is a projection of human psychopathology. The Hebrew prophets may have been compelled to use the image of a punishing God because it was the only one that people would take seriously. Even though the prophets made it clear that God wanted only good for his children, and that their rebelliousness was blocking his intentions for good, modern readers often cannot get past the judgmental severity. But we can now recognize that it was an *image*, useful in its day, but able to be surpassed by images that are more reflective of the non-narcissistic nature of God's parental attitude.

We can no longer tolerate any concept of God that is inconsistent with the attitude of an infinitely wise and loving parent. The popular atonement concept involves a stern Father and a compassionate Son coming to an agreement about transferring to the Son the severe penalty deserved by the human race. This is unworthy of the gospel, since it assumes a Father who is either bad or weak—either a narcissistic father who demands some kind of sacrificial victim to appease his honor, or a weak father who is powerless in the face of a law that requires a victim. But God is the source of universal law and is not powerless in the face of any law, certainly not one supposedly requiring violence. There is no law to which God is forced to conform. That

19. Matt 9:22; Mark 5:34; 10:52; Luke 7:50; 8:48; 17:19; 18:42. As we saw in chapter 1, the Greek *sesōken* can mean "made well," "healed," or "saved."

would make God less than God. God's volition is not secondary to *anything* else in the divine nature.

Anything in our theology that attributes weakness or cruelty to God is inconsistent with our highest ideals of parental love and must be rejected. God is at least as careful and considerate as any earthly parent. "Your heavenly Father knows that you need all these things" (Matt 6:32).

The Christian architects of the atonement doctrine were not setting out to distort the gospel. Rather, they were trying to present the gospel *vividly*, and nothing was so vivid as ideas that drew upon sacrificial thinking at a time when the most serious religions practiced sacrificial rituals. Christian atonement doctrine did replace animal sacrifice but it shaped and perpetuated a certain sacrificial mentality. Sacrifice is fundamentally manipulative and anxiety-driven, whether we look at it as propitiatory or as cleansing. If propitiatory, it is assuming a violent God who can be appeased or paid off with a costly sacrifice. If cleansing, it assumes a magical cleansing power of blood. Such superstitions come from the childhood of the human race. The Father of whom Jesus spoke does not need to be placated, nor does imaginary impurity need to be ritually purged.

The manipulative psychology of trying to appease God arises out of childhood strategies for coping with brutal parents. Abuse victims commonly practice a strategy of payment through suffering. Frightened children develop strategies of diversion and avoidance, ways of shifting blame or of hiding. If we are to emerge into ethical and mature thinking, we must recognize such ideas as harmful. We need our approach to God to be very different from any kind of approach to a violent parent.

Stated otherwise, Western theology has tended to impose a rigid soterio-logic that resembles the logic of Roman law[20] and makes salvation look like a legal trick rather than life-changing transformation (new creation! 2 Cor 5:17) and discovery (buried treasure! Matt 13:44). Salvation is new life.

What Salvation?

The salvation Jesus brought is not derived from some magical transaction that took place through a political killing carried out to mollify some religious professionals who felt threatened by an independent religious

---

20. Ever since Tertullian, rationalizing theology has drawn upon *"explanatory models drawn from Roman law"* (Simpson, "Atonement and Sacrifice," 69).

teacher. Those things are *human*; salvation is *divine*. Jesus offered salvation and healing long before he was killed. He healed the outcasts and the blind and restored self-respect to people who were despised or despised themselves; he forgave sins.

It is not *what was done* to Jesus that matters, it is *who Jesus was*—and *is*—that matter. The crucifixion is not the location of salvation; *Jesus* is . . . and God's generosity is, and our faith is. These three are connected: the downreach of God, the outreach of the Revealer (the Son), and the upreach of our faith. Salvation is a reception of life. Faith taps into the life of God, and more specifically into the power of the actual life-giver, Jesus, who is the creator or cocreator. Jesus is the creator of "all things" or of "the worlds" in John 1:3; 1 Cor 8:6; Col 1:16; Heb 1:2. Actually, all four passages say that things exist or came into being *through* him. Jesus is a cocreator with God, or even *for* God. *This* is why Jesus has the power of healing and life. He is the Creator, the agent of God, and the embodiment of the Divine. As Son of God, he is both our elder brother and our father. As the designer of life, the creator of worlds, he is our father. This father says "let the little children come to me" (Mark 10:14) and "you will be children of the Most High" (Luke 6:35). With such a role model, let no one ever again denigrate the role of fatherhood.

Traumatized by, but also fascinated with, the spectacle of violence, and feeling guilty about it, theologians were moved to form mythologies of meaning about the crucifixion, momentarily forgetting that God was offering salvation *before* the crucifixion and that this ugly example of human cowardice and violence was unnecessary.

God saves us *despite* the crucifixion, not *because* of it. The cross shows how humanity *resisted* the message of salvation that God continuously offered, despite human evasiveness and fear. The cross was a shameful, not a magical event, but somehow it commanded human attention in a way that nothing else did. Human infatuation with violence, morbidity, and mystery, have made the cross the avenue for communicating *something* (though corrupted with mythology) about the Son of Man. Jesus preferred to communicate his message openly and without mystery—"day after day I was with you in the temple teaching" (Mark 14:49)—reaching people through their honest spiritual hunger instead of through a teaching that blended spirituality with morbid religious imagination. Even today, many Christians become sentimental only about the Master's tortured death and not about the revelation of God *throughout* his life, which was full of many fascinating encounters, and should inspire us as much as the story of his death. We cannot appreciate the courage and unselfishness that he brought to the cross unless we appreciate the love and wisdom that he revealed every day, and unless we recognize that the offer of salvation was openly offered before—and unrelated to—the events leading to his death.

It may be, however, that Jesus allowed his death to become a vehicle for his teachings, knowing that the story of his death would reach more people than he would be able to reach in person once the religious authorities had decided to block his efforts. Jesus *would* have taken Jerusalem under his wings as a mother hen does her chicks, but she was not willing, and so he had to resort to plan B. He does seem to have arranged things in such a way that the story about his life, death, and resurrection would have the maximum effect. Before his death, he had already given a number of sermons in the temple area, and had assaulted the Sadducees' sacrificial industry, so no one was unaware of his prophetic activity nor of who wanted him out of the way. He managed to arrange his death for Passover Day and signaled (at the Last Supper) the founding a new community, based on the founding of a new community after the first Passover.[21] He had managed to train his apostles, but they were not courageous enough to get themselves killed yet. This bought some time for the teachings to sink in, the story to spread, the Spirit to start doing its work, and the movement to grow.

To test this idea (that Jesus would resort to a plan B that was not his preferred method), I look at his service to needy people. He would have preferred that they focus on the miracle of spiritual healing more than on any physical healings, yet he was willing to cure people who had a superstitious mentality. He must have known they would become infatuated with the healing miracle (Matt 9:28–31) and "proclaim it freely" (Mark 1:45), yet he was willing to allow this to happen. Most people's religious thinking was infected with magical cure-seeking, which is intellectually immature. Yet Jesus allowed them to project their magical thinking onto him, to use him as a crutch or even an idol, in the long period before they would eventually outgrow magical thinking. He cured people even though he knew that they would become infatuated with the miracle and would continue to think superstitiously. Come to me all you who are heavy-laden—even

21. In Exodus 24, Moses uses a covenant sacrifice to mark the founding of a new community. A covenant sacrifice is not purificatory or substitutionary but involves a self-curse, implying "if I break this covenant, may the same happen to me as happened to this animal." What Jesus is highlighting is the formation of a community with which he will drink and dine again in the afterlife.

with psychological trauma and infantile thinking—and I will give you rest[22] (while waiting for you to grow up philosophically).

Perhaps this finds a parallel in the arena of doctrine—that Jesus is willing to endure infantile doctrines and superstitious teachings, while waiting for us to outgrow them. This is, indeed, a kind and parental attitude, tolerating childish behavior as long as there some sign of growth. Jesus even rejoiced that, regarding "deeds of power," the Father had "revealed them to infants" (Matt 11:23, 25), and that praise was coming "out of the mouths of infants" (Matt 21:16). This returns us to our initial message, that one must become like a child to enter the kingdom of heaven (Matt 18:3). This also forces the observation that mature believers should have the attitude of a patient parent toward childish doctrinal formulations, rather than being judgmental like the rigid son in the prodigal son story.

Unselfish service, then, is where all this leads.

"Do not let your left hand know what your right hand is doing"

This saying (Matt 6:3) signifies self-forgetful giving, not giving alms in order to be seen by others or to gain spiritual prestige.

The religiosity of Jesus differs from the religiosity of all other religions and philosophies in that he does not ask for increasing self-examination, which leads to subtle religious narcissism. Rather, Jesus directs us outward, to serve others, and not to obsess about our own spiritual condition. In Jesus' teaching, self-formation is unconscious, and it happens through serving others. Healthy parenting is, of course, an intense service activity. Parenting, theology, and psychology can be of mutual assistance to each other, all in service to the ideal of the family of God.

The gospel's family metaphor needs to become more prominent in Christian discourse, so that we cease to overlook the fundamentals: the health and flourishing of all members of this huge cosmic family. It often is difficult to love humanity. Jesus' term for people was "sheep," nothing worse. They are clueless and they need shepherds; they are vulnerable and needy, so "feed my lambs . . . . tend my sheep" (John 21:15–16).

22. Matt 11:28.

Ethics in the Jesus Community

Jesus established a positive system of religious ethics, an anti-patronal banquet, an anti-exhibitionist religious life, and an anti-selfish approach to religion which yet was of unparalleled benefit to the self. The self-forgetfulness of Jesus was miles away from self-conscious asceticism and self-punishing monasticism. The self-forgetfulness of Jesus is the secret to finding the self in community.

Ethics needs to build upon the foundations that Jesus put in place: the supremacy of God, the three-step rule for dealing with unruly members of the congregation (Matt 18:15–17), helping the person wounded in the ditch without regard to his status or to yours (Luke 10:30–37), letting go of worldly attachments, making your shrines houses of prayer for all people (Mark 11:17).

What healing is there for diseased humanity apart from the healing of both individuals and communities? Trying to heal the individual alone will only heighten the loneliness and potential victimization of these recovering, but unsocialized, individuals. Trying to create the perfect community can end up suppressing the individual and creating an anti-intellectual sect. We need both the mind and creativity of the individual and the ethics and pleasing interaction with others that we get in community.

The ethics of Jesus allow for self-finding through self-forgetting. There is a profound trust underlying such an apparently risky strategy. Even deeply religious people are often not prepared to trust others and to accept uncertainty to such a degree. Some hesitate to trust the socialization process when there is no authoritarian control. Others will not trust any group at all. We need to outgrow these extremes and realize that group process need not be authoritarian. Individuals always have to surrender something when they join groups, but they should not be asked to surrender their ability to think or their honest commitment to values. The only groups that will prosper are ones with honestly value-motivated individuals.

We need to remember that "God sets the solitary in families" (Ps 68:6 NKJV). God not only saves the individual, but also sets brothers in *active* brotherly relationship with others.

I have tended to set this ethical-spiritual approach in opposition to the doctrinal and authoritarian approach of atonement-heavy theologies. It is also possible to do an end-run around negative theology without confronting it, and others have done this. Scot McKnight has written a book insisting that atonement not be discussed apart from kingdom,[23] that is, apart from the new community that compassionate self-giving sets out to create. He is really not talking about atonement *doctrine* at all but about the ethical spiritual notion of at-one-ment, which is indeed the origin of our *English* word "atonement." It may be that McKnight's transformation of language and positive shifting of focus will be more effective than my confrontation of atonement ideas. Most likely, both approaches are needed. The American Revolution needed both the radical Thomas Paine and the level-headed John Adams.

Infantilizing the Congregation

Of course, the mere expression of the family principle in a church community does not eliminate the possibility of pathology. There are many ways the family principle can be distorted, given sufficient lack of character development in the congregation, controlling behavior by the minister, or dishonesty by both members and minister. Unhealthy churches are at least as common as unhealthy families. In fact, church structure often encourages grandiosity in the minister and infantilism in the members.

Many ministers are lords more than ministers, pontificators more than helpers. It is high time that believers started puncturing the narcissistic bubbles of some pastors. But before they can do this, they must first puncture their own trance of narcissistic neediness, which enshrined the domineering pastor in the first place. Therefore what is most needed is more *progress* toward courageous and responsible religious living, no longer passively accepting the word of religious authorities.

Only genuine firsthand religious living will empower the congregation, forcing the minister down off his or her pedestal, and lifting the congregation up out of its mindless passivity. Do we love God with our *minds* as well as with our hearts and souls?

23. McKnight, *A Community Called Atonement*, 13.

Bibliography

1 Enoch. See Isaac, E.

Albertz, Rainer. *A History of Israelite Religion in the Old Testament Period, Volume I: From the Beginnings to the End of the Monarchy*. Translated by John Bowden. OTL. Louisville: Westminster John Knox, 1994.

Anderson, Paul N., Felix Just, and Tom Thatcher, eds. *John, Jesus, and History, Volume 1: Critical Appraisals of Critical Views*. SBLSymS 44. Atlanta: SBL, 2007.

Bailey, Kenneth E. "Informal Controlled Oral Tradition and the Synoptic Gospels." *AJT* 5/1 (1991) 34–54.

Bailey, Michael J., David Bobrow, Marilyn Wolfe, and Sarah Mikach. "Sexual Orientation of Adult Sons of Gay Fathers." *Developmental Psychology* 31 (1995) 124–29.

Balch, David L. "Paul, Families, and Households." In *Paul in the Greco-Roman World: A Handbook*, edited by J. Paul Sampley, 258–92. Harrisburg: Trinity, 2003.

Barclay, John M. G. "The Family as the Bearer of Religion." In *Constructing Early Christian Families: Family As Social Reality and Metaphor*, edited by Halvor Moxnes, 66–80. London: Routledge, 1997.

———. "There is Neither Old Nor Young?" *NTS* 53 (2007) 225–41.

Barton, Stephen C. *Discipleship and Family Ties in Mark and Matthew*. Cambridge: Cambridge University Press, 1994.

———. "The Relativization of Family Ties in the Jewish and Graeco-Roman Traditions." In *Constructing Early Christian Families: Family As Social Reality and Metaphor*, edited by Halvor Moxnes, 81–100. London: Routledge, 1997.

Bell, Daniel A. *Beyond Liberal Democracy: Political Thinking for an East Asian Context*. Princeton: Princeton University Press, 2006.

Bellah, Robert N., Richard Madsen, William M. Sullivan, Ann Swidler, and Steven M. Tipton. *Habits of the Heart: Individualism and Commitment in American Life*. Berkeley: University of California Press, 1985.

Berthrong, John H. *All Under Heaven: Transforming Paradigms in Confucian-Christian Dialogue*. Albany: State University of New York Press, 1994.

Bigner, Jerry, and Brooke Jacobsen. "Parenting Behaviors of Homosexual and Heterosexual Fathers." *Journal of Homosexuality* 18 (1989) 173–86.

Blankenhorn, David. "Foreword: The Person of the Father." In *Calling God "Father,"* by John Miller, ix–xiv. New York: Paulist, 1999.

Brightman, Edgar Sheffield. *The Spiritual Life*. Nashville: Abingdon-Cokesbury, 1942.

Browning, Don S. *Equality and the Family: A Fundamental, Practical Theology of Children, Mothers, and Fathers in Modern Societies*. Grand Rapids: Eerdmans, 2007.

————. "Introduction: The Equal-Regard Family in Context." In *The Equal-Regard Family and Its Friendly Critics: Don Browning and the Practical Theological Ethics of the Family*, edited by John Witte Jr., M. Christian Green, and Amy Wheeler, 1–16. Grand Rapids: Eerdmans, 2007.

————. *Marriage and Modernization: How Globalization Threatens Marriage and What to Do About It*. Religion, Marriage, and Family. Grand Rapids: Eerdmans, 2003.

Bushnell, Horace. *Christian Nurture*. New Haven: Yale University Press, 1916; originally published in 1861.

Byrskog, Samuel. "A New Perspective on the Jesus Tradition: Reflections on James D. G. Dunn's *Jesus Remembered*." *Journal for the Study of the New Testament* 26 (2004) 459–71.

Cahill, Lisa Sowle. *Between the Sexes: Foundations for a Christian Ethics of Sexuality*. Philadelphia: Fortress, 1985.

Capps, Donald. "The Decades of Life: Relocating Erikson's Stages." *Pastoral Psychology* 53 (2004) 3–32.

————. *Life Cycle Theory and Pastoral Care*. Eugene, OR: Wipf & Stock, 2002.

Carroll R., M. Daniel. "Family in the Prophetic Literature." In *Family in the Bible: Exploring Customs, Culture, in Context*, edited by Richard S. Hess and M. Daniel Carroll R., 100–122. Grand Rapids: Baker, 2003.

Dixon, Suzanne. *The Roman Ramily*. Ancient Society and History. Baltimore: Johns Hopkins University Press, 1992.

Dorrien, Gary. *The Making of American Liberal Theology: Imagining Progressive Religion, 1805–1900*. Louisville: Westminster John Knox, 2001.

Dostoyevsky, Fyodor. *The Brothers Karamazov*. Translated by Andrew R. MacAndrew. New York: Bantam, 1970.

Dumas, Jean E., and Jenelle Nissley-Tsiopinis. "Parental Global Religiousness, Sanctification of Parenting, and Positive and Negative Religious Coping as Predictors of Parental and Child Functioning." *The International Journal for the Psychology of Religion* 16 (2006) 289–310.

Dunn, James D. G. *Jesus Remembered*. Christianity in the Making 1. Grand Rapids: Eerdmans, 2003.

————. *A New Perspective on Jesus: What the Quest for the Historical Jesus Missed*. Grand Rapids: Baker, 2005.

————. *Romans 1–8*. WBC 38A. Dallas: Word, 1988.

————. *The Theology of Paul the Apostle*. Grand Rapids: Eerdmans, 1998.

Enoch. See Isaac, E.

Erikson, Erik H. *Childhood and Society*. 2nd ed. New York: Norton, 1963.

————. *Identity and the Life Cycle*. 2nd ed. New York: Norton, 1980.

————. *The Life Cycle Completed*. New York: Norton, 1982.

————. *Toys and Reasons*. New York: Norton, 1977.

Ferm, Deane. *Contemporary American Theologies: A Critical Survey*. New York: Seabury, 1981.

Finlan, Stephen. *The Apostle Paul and the Pauline Tradition*. Collegeville, MN: Liturgical, 2008.

————. "Deification in Jesus' Teaching." In *Theōsis: Deification in Modern Theology*, vol. 2, edited by Vladimir Kharlamov, 21–41. Eugene: Pickwick, 2011.

————. *Options on Atonement in Christian Thought*. Collegeville, MN: Liturgical, 2007.

Flacelière, Robert. *Daily Life in Greece at the Time of Pericles.* Phoenix Press Daily Life. Translated by Peter Green. London: Phoenix, 1965; French original 1959.

Fowler, James W. *Stages of Faith: The Psychology of Human Development and the Quest for Meaning.* San Francisco: Harper, 1981.

Francis, James. "Children and Childhood in the New Testament." In *The Family in Theological Perspective,* edited by Stephen C. Barton, 65–85. Edinburgh: T. & T. Clark, 1996.

Friedman, Edwin H. *Generation to Generation: Family Process in Church and Synagogue.* New York: Guilford, 1985.

Garnsey, Peter, and Richard Saller. *The Roman Empire: Economy, Society, and Culture.* Berkeley: University of California Press, 1987.

Gerhardsson, Birger. "Illuminating the Kingdom: Narrative Meshalim in the Synoptic Gospels." In *Jesus and the Oral Gospel Tradition,* edited by Henry Wansbrough, 266–309. JSNT Sup 64. Sheffield, UK: JSOT, 1991.

Gilder, George. *Men and Marriage.* Revised and expanded edition of *Sexual Suicide.* Gretna, LA: Pelican, 1986.

Gilligan, Carol. *In a Different Voice: Psychological Theory and Women's Development.* Cambridge, MA: Harvard University Press, 1993.

Girard, René. *Evolution and Conversion: Dialogues on the Origins of Culture.* London: T. & T. Clark, 2007.

———. *Things Hidden Since the Foundation of the World.* London: Athlone, 1987.

Glaser, Chris. *As My Own Soul: The Blessing of Same-Gender Marriage.* New York: Seabury, 2009.

Glenn, Norval, et al. *Why Marriage Matters: Twenty-One Conclusions from the Social Sciences.* New York: Institute for American Values, 2002.

Granberg-Michaelson, Karin. "Parenting and Reparenting." *Sojourners* 8/2 (1979) 30–34.

Greer, Rowan A. *Broken Lights and Mended Lives: Theology and Common Life in the Early Church.* University Park: Pennsylvania State University Press, 1986.

Greven, Philip. *Spare the Child: The Religious Roots of Punishment and the Psychological Impact of Physical Abuse.* New York: Knopf, 1991.

Gundry-Volf, Judith M. "The Least and the Greatest: Children in the New Testament." In *The Child in Christian Thought,* edited by Marcia J. Bunge, 29–60. Grand Rapids: Eerdmans, 2001.

Hanson, K. C. "The Herodians and Mediterranean Kinship; Part I: Genealogy and Descent." *Biblical Theology Bulletin* 19 (1989) 75–84.

———. "Readers Guide: Kinship." *Biblical Theology Bulletin* 24 (1994) 183–94.

Hanson, K. C., and Douglas E. Oakman. *Palestine in the Time of Jesus: Social Structures and Social Conflicts.* Minneapolis: Fortress, 1998.

Hellerman, Joseph H. *The Ancient Church as Family.* Minneapolis: Fortress, 2001.

———. "Brothers and Friends in Philippi: Family Honor in the Roman World and in Paul's Letter to the Philippians." *Biblical Theology Bulletin* 39 (2009) 15–25.

Hendel, Ronald S. "Prophets, Priests, and the Efficacy of Ritual." In *Pomegranates and Golden Bells: Studies in Biblical, Jewish, and Near Eastern Ritual, Law, and Literature in Honor of Jacob Milgrom,* edited by David P. Wright, David Noel Freedman, and Avi Hurvitz, 185–98. Winona Lake, IN: Eisenbrauns, 1995.

Herzog, James H. "On Father Hunger: The Father's Role in the Modulation of Aggressive Drive and Fantasy." In *Father and Child: Developmental and Clinical Perspectives,* edited by Stanley H. Cath, Alan R. Gurwitt, and John Munder Ross, 163–74. Boston: Little Brown, 1982.

Horrell, David G. *The Social Ethos of the Corinthian Correspondence: Interests and Ideology from 1 Corinthians to 1 Clement*. Edinburgh: T. & T. Clark, 1996.

Isaac, E. Translation of *1 Enoch* in *The Old Testament Pseudepigrapha* 1:13–89. Edited by James H. Charlesworth. New York: Doubleday, 1983.

Jordan, Mark D. *Blessing Same-Sex Unions: The Perils of Queer Romance and the Confusions of Christian Marriage*. Chicago: University of Chicago Press, 2005.

Keener, Craig S. *Paul, Women and Wives: Marriage and Women's Ministry in the Letters of Paul*. Peabody, MA: Hendrickson, 1992.

Kitto, H. D. F. *The Greeks*. Rev. ed. Baltimore: Penguin, 1957.

Kohlberg, Lawrence. *The Philosophy of Moral Development: Moral Stages and the Idea of Justice*. San Francisco: Harper & Row, 1981.

Lasch, Christopher. *Haven in a Heartless World: The Family Besieged*. New York: Basic, 1977.

Lasine, Stuart. "Divine Narcissism and Yahweh's Parenting Style." *BibInt* 10 (2002) 36–56.

Lee, Dorothy Ann. "The Symbol of Divine Fatherhood." *Semeia* 85 (1999) 177–87.

Levine, Amy-Jill. "Theological Education, the Bible, and History: Détente in the Culture Wars." In *Early Christian Families in Context: An Interdisciplinary Dialogue*, edited by David L. Balch and Carolyn Osiek, 327–36. Grand Rapids: Eerdmans, 2003.

Louden, Robert B. "'What Does Heaven Say?' Christian Wolff and Western Interpretation of Confucian Ethics." In *Confucius and the Analects: New Essays*, edited by Bryan W. Van Norden, 73–93. Oxford: Oxford University Press, 2002.

MacDonald, Margaret Y. "Was Celsus Right? The Role of Women in the Expansion of Early Christianity." In *Early Christian Families in Context: An Interdisciplinary Dialogue*, edited by David L. Balch and Carolyn Osiek, 157–84. Grand Rapids: Eerdmans, 2003.

Malina, Bruce J. *The Social Gospel of Jesus: The Kingdom of God in Mediterranean Perspective*. Minneapolis: Fortress, 2001.

Mathews, Shailer. *Jesus on Social Institutions*. Philadelphia: Fortress, 1971.

McKnight, Scot. *A Community Called Atonement*. Living Theology. Nashville: Abingdon, 2007.

McLanahan, Sara. *Growing Up with a Single Parent: What Hurts, What Helps*. Cambridge, MA: Harvard University Press, 1994.

Meyer, Jeffery F. "Confucian 'Familism' in America." In *American Religions and the Family: How Faith Traditions Cope with Modernization and Democracy*, edited by Don S. Browning and David A. Clairmont. New York: Columbia University Press, 2007.

Meyers, Carol. *Discovering Eve: Ancient Israelite Women in Context*. New York: Oxford University Press, 1988.

Miller, John W. *Calling God "Father": Essays on the Bible, Fatherhood and Culture*. New York: Paulist, 1999.

Miller-McLemore, Bonnie J. *Let the Children Come: Reimagining Childhood from a Christian Perspective*. San Francisco: Jossey-Bass, 2003.

Morgan, Patricia. *Farewell to the Family? Public Policy and Family Breakdown in Britain and the USA*. London: Health and Welfare Unit of the Institute of Economic Affairs, 1995.

Moxnes, Halvor. "What is Family? Problems in Constructing Early Christian Families." In *Constructing Early Christian Families: Family As Social Reality and Metaphor*, edited by Halvor Moxnes, 13–41. London: Routledge, 1997.

Murray-Swank, Aaron, Annette Mahoney, and Kenneth I. Pargament. "Sanctification of Parenting: Links to Corporal Punishment and Parental Warmth among Biblically Conservative and Liberal Mothers." *The International Journal for the Psychology of Religion* 16 (2006) 271–87.

Newman, Jay. *Biblical Religion and Family Values: A Problem in the Philosophy of Culture*. Westport, CT: Praeger, 2001.

Osiek, Carolyn. "Female Slaves, *Porneia*, and the Limits of Obedience." In *Early Christian Families in Context: An Interdisciplinary Dialogue*, edited by David L. Balch and Carolyn Osiek, 255–74. Grand Rapids: Eerdmans, 2003.

Osiek, Carolyn, and David L. Balch. *Families in the New Testament World: Households and House Churches*. Family, Religion and Culture. Louisville: Westminster John Knox, 1997.

Outka, Gene. *Agape: An Ethical Analysis*. New Haven, CT: Yale University Press, 1972.

Parker, Stephen, and Yvonne Bissonnette Tate. "Using Erikson's Developmental Theory to Understand and Nurture Spiritual Development in Christians." *Journal of Psychology and Christianity* 26 (2007) 218–26.

Perdue, Leo G. "The Household, Old Testament Theology, and Contemporary Hermeneutics." In *Families in Ancient Israel*, by Leo G. Perdue, Joseph Blenkinsopp, John J. Collins, and Carol Meyers, 223-57. Family, Religion and Culture. Louisville: Westminster John Knox, 1997.

———. "The Israelite and Early Jewish Family: Summary and Conclusions." In *Families in Ancient Israel*, by Leo G. Perdue, Joseph Blenkinsopp, John J. Collins, and Carol Meyers, 163–222. Family, Religion and Culture. Louisville: Westminster John Knox, 1997.

Plato. *Laws, Vol. 1, Books 1-6*. Translated by Robert Gregg Bury. In *Plato, Volume X*. Loeb Classical Library. London: Heinemann, 1926.

Pope, Stephen J. "The Place of Evolutionary Psychology in a Practical Theological Ethics of Families." In *The Equal-Regard Family and Its Friendly Critics: Don Browning and the Practical Theological Ethics of the Family*, edited by John Witte Jr., M. Christian Green, and Amy Wheeler, 56–68. Grand Rapids: Eerdmans, 2007.

Popenoe, David, *Disturbing the Nest: Family Change and Decline in Modern Societies*. New York: de Gruyter, 1988.

———. *Life without Father: Compelling New Evidence that Fatherhood and Marriage Are Indispensable for the Good of Children and Society*. New York: Martin Kessler, 1996.

Porter, Stanley E. "Family in the Epistles." In *Family in the Bible: Exploring Customs, Culture, in Context*, edited by Richard S. Hess and M. Daniel Carroll R., 148–66. Grand Rapids: Baker, 2003.

Riesner, Rainer. "Jesus as Preacher and Teacher." In *Jesus and the Oral Gospel Tradition*, edited by Henry Wansbrough, 185-210. JSNT Sup 64. Sheffield: JSOT, 1991.

Rubio, Julie Hanlon. *A Christian Theology of Marriage and Family*. New York: Paulist, 2003.

Saller, Richard. *Patriarchy, Property and Death in the Roman Family*. Cambridge Studies in Population, Economy and Society in Past Time 25. Cambridge: Cambridge University Press, 1994.

Sandage, Steven J., and F. LeRon Shults. *Transforming Spirituality: Integrating Theology and Psychology*. Grand Rapids: Baker, 2006.

Scheler, Max. "The Forms of Knowledge and Culture." In *Philosophical Perspectives*, 13–49. Translated by Oscar A. Haac. Beacon Hill, MA: Beacon, 1958.

Schüssler Fiorenza, Elisabeth. *In Memory of Her: A Feminist Theological Reconstruction of Christian Origins*. 10th anniversary edition. New York: Crossroad, 1994.

Shults, F. LeRon. See Steven J. Sandage.

Simpson, Theo. "Atonement and Sacrifice: The De-Ideologization of Western Christianity." *Journal of Theology for Southern Africa* 128 (2007) 53–70.

Snarey, John R. *How Fathers Care for the Next Generation: A Four-Decade Study*. Cambridge, MA: Harvard University Press, 1993.

Snodgrass, Klyne. "The Gospel of Jesus." In *The Written Gospel*, edited by Markus Bockmuehl and Donald A. Hagner, 31–44. Cambridge: Cambridge University Press, 2005.

Song, Young I. *Battered Women in Korean Immigrant Families: The Silent Scream*. New York: Garland, 1996.

Stanton, Graham. *Gospel Truth? New Light on Jesus and the Gospels*. Valley Forge, PA: Trinity, 1995.

Stark, Rodney. *The Rise of Christianity*. San Francisco: HarperCollins, 1997.

Teilhard de Chardin, Pierre. *The Divine Milieu*. New York: Harper & Row, 1960; originally Paris, 1957.

———. *Human Energy*. Translated by J. M. Cohen. London: Collins, 1969.

Tennis, Diane. *Is God the Only Reliable Father?* Philadelphia: Westminster, 1985.

Thatcher, Adrian. *Theology and Families*. Challenges in Contemporary Theology. Oxford: Blackwell, 2007.

Thompson, Dorothy J. "The Hellenistic Family." In *The Cambridge Companion to the Hellenistic World*, edited by Glenn R. Bugh, 93–112. Cambridge: Cambridge University Press, 2006.

Tillich, Paul. *The Courage to Be*. New Haven, CT: Yale University Press, 1952.

———. *Dynamics of Faith*. New York: Harper, 2001.

Troeltsch, Ernst. *The Social Teaching of the Christian Churches*. Translated by Olive Wyon. New York: Harper, 1960.

Van Norden, Bryan W. "Introduction." In *Confucius and the Analects: New Essays*, edited by Bryan W. Van Norden, 3-36. Oxford: Oxford University Press, 2002.

Viladesau, Richard, and Mark Massa, *World Religions: A Sourcebook for Students of Christian Theology*. Mahwah, NJ: Paulist, 1994.

Waite, Linda J., and Maggie Gallagher. *The Case for Marriage: Why Married People Are Happier, Healthier, and Better off Financially*. New York: Doubleday, 2000.

Wall, John, Don Browning, William J. Doherty, and Stephen Posts, eds. *Marriage, Health and the Professions: If Marriage Is Good For You, What Does This Mean for Law, Medicine, Ministry, Therapy, Business?* Cambridge, MA: Eerdmans, 2002.

Waters, Brent. *The Family in Christian Social and Political Thought*. Oxford Studies in Theological Ethics. Oxford: Oxford University Press, 2007.

Watts, Alan. *Nature, Man and Woman*. New York: Vintage, 1970.

Wenham, Gordon J. "Family in the Pentateuch." In *Family in the Bible: Exploring Customs, Culture, in Context*, edited by Richard S. Hess and M. Daniel Carroll R., 17–31. Grand Rapids: Baker, 2003.

Westfall, Cynthia Long. "Family in the Gospels and Acts." In *Family in the Bible: Exploring Customs, Culture, in Context,* edited by Richard S. Hess and M. Daniel Carroll R. Grand Rapids: Baker, 2003.

Westphal, Merold. *Overcoming Onto-Theology: Toward a Postmodern Christian Faith.* Perspectives in Continental Philosophy. New York: Fordham University Press, 2001.

Wilson, Edward O. *On Human Nature.* Cambridge: Cambridge University Press, 1978.

Wolfe, Alan. *Whose Keeper? Social Science and Moral Obligation.* Berkeley: University of California Press, 1989.

Wright, N. T. *Jesus and the Victory of God.* Minneapolis: Fortress, 1996.

Yao, Xinzhong. *An Introduction to Confucianism.* Cambridge: Cambridge University Press, 2000.

Young, Pamela Dickey. "The Fatherhood of God at the Turn of Another Millennium." *Semeia* 85 (1999) 195–202.

Young, Frances. *The Theology of the Pastoral Epistles.* NT Theology. Cambridge: Cambridge University Press, 1994.

Index of Names and Subjects

Index of Scripture

Ephesians (*continued*)

5:21–6:9	4
5:22–27	54
5:23–24	59
5:25	59
6:1	59
6:4	59
6:5	59
6:9	59
6:21	54

Philippians

1:6	24
1:9	10
1:9–10	52
2:13	24
4:1–3	4
4:2–3	57

Colossians

1:16	88
3:18	59
3:19	59
3:20	59
3:21	29, 59
4:1	59

1 Timothy

1:7	57
2:6	85
2:8–15	4
2:11–15	55
2:12	57, 67
2:15	54–55
3:4	66
3:15	58
4:3	55
4:7	55, 57
4:13	60
5:4	54
5:8	58

5:11–14	57
5:13–14	55
5:14	54
5:23	55
6:1–9	4

2 Timothy

3:6	4, 57
3:6–7	55
4:3	57

Titus

1:11	4
2:1–10	4
2:3	57
2:3–5	55
2:5	4, 57
2:9	4

Philemon

4–7	62
8	62
9	62
12	61
14	62
15–16	62
16	50, 62
17	61
19	62
21	62

Hebrews

1:2	88
9:22–28	85

James

1:27	85
4:8	85